FEAR NOT!

THE TRUE STORY OF A CANCER SURVIVOR WHO WAS HEALED AND TRANSFORMED BY GOD

W0010965

LISA WEST

with Elena Bennett

Foreword by Dr. W. Perry Ballard, III

Published by Lighten Media Group

ISBN: 978-1-7329218-0-1

Scripture quotations marked (NASB) are from the NEW AMERICAN STANDARD BIBLE®, Copyright © 1960, 1962, 1963, 1968, 1971, 1972, 1973, 1975, 1977, 1995 by The Lockman Foundation. Used by permission.

Scripture quotations marked (ESV) are from the The Holy Bible, English Standard Version. ESV® Text Edition: 2016. Copyright © 2001 by Crossway Bibles, a publishing ministry of Good News Publishers.

Scripture quotations marked (NIV) are from THE HOLY BIBLE, NEW INTERNATIONAL VERSION®, NIV® Copyright © 1973, 1978, 1984, 2011 by Biblica, Inc.® Used by permission. All rights reserved worldwide.

Scripture quotations marked (KJV) are from the King James Version (public domain).

Please note that certain translations do not capitalize references to God. However, the author has chosen to capitalize all such references to honor Him.

Interior Layout: James Armstrong, UpWrite Publishing

Cover Design: Michael Sean Allen

November 2018 Edition

This book is dedicated to the memory of my beloved father and all-time hero—Joseph B. Dodd. Because of the unconditional, unwavering love you always showed me, and the constant faith and trust you always had in me, I was able to have complete faith and trust in a Higher parental authority—my Heavenly Father. Thanks, Dad, for that, and for everything you taught me.

I also dedicate this book to my children and their spouses, and to my existing and future grandchildren. I hope it provides all of you with a better understanding of how I came to believe in Jesus Christ as my personal Lord and Savior, and why my faith in Him will never waiver or cease. It also is my hope that each generation that follows me will continue to pass this book on to the next.

Contents

Preface

> *"For I the LORD thy God will hold thy right hand, saying unto thee, 'FEAR NOT';*
> *I will help thee."*
> — Isaiah 41:13 (KJV; emphasis added)

THE PHRASE "FEAR NOT" is mentioned in the Bible 365 times, which interestingly enough, equates to once for each day of the year. Obviously (at least to me), God realized that fear was a human emotion that often consumed and crippled His children—thus preventing them from believing and having faith in Him. I think God knew that we needed a constant reminder throughout the Bible to "Fear Not!"

The dictionary definition of fear is: a distressing emotion aroused by impending danger, evil, pain or other threats to one's well-being. Whether the threat is real or imagined, the feeling or condition of being afraid can be paralyzing.

The spiritual or religious definition of fear is: (1) the inversion or opposite of faith in God—that is, the belief in evil versus good; and (2) a debilitating emotion that comes from the enemy, Satan, who strives to separate us from God, prevent us from serving Him, and keep us from fulfilling our potential and His will for our lives.

Satan loves it when he holds us in a tightly wrapped cocoon of fear. God loves it when we break through Satan's bondage of fear through unwavering faith in His Son, Jesus Christ, His great grace and His awesome powers. Only with such faith in God are we able to break through the slavery of fear and emerge transformed—and as free as a butterfly.

Fear controlled every aspect of my life until I found true faith in God in my 40s—which grew even more in my 50s with a trial that tested my faith to its outermost limits: cancer. From that, I absolutely knew that with God, all things are possible—including the spiritual healing of my many fears that kept me from service and obedience to God, as well as my complete physical healing.

It is my hope that those who are facing a frightening trial in life know that they can call upon the Lord to replace their fear with faith in Him. And once you have solid faith in God, you can stand firm in it, knowing that God will fight your battle with and for you.

"I sought the LORD, and He answered me, and delivered me from all my fears."
– Psalm 34:4 (NASB)

Introduction

On Super Bowl Sunday of 2010—February 7 to be exact—I had an encounter with the Lord.

That experience was like something straight out of a science-fiction movie. But it was 100 percent real. And, my husband and oldest daughter witnessed it.

The morning after my encounter with God, I could no longer feel the very large and hard, rapidly growing tumor in my left breast that was diagnosed only six weeks earlier as Clinical Stage 3 and Grade 3 cancer. Nor could my oncologist palpate it while I was lying on his exam table the next day, just before only the third round of my prescribed chemotherapy.

While that healing was certainly the most dramatic and awesome miracle that I experienced during my battle with cancer, it was far from the only one. I was never nauseous, sick or hospitalized with infections from the brutal

1

chemo regimen that I was prescribed—which completely debilitates most. Despite that, I always had the energy to exercise daily and carry on with my normal activities. I had a good appetite, and maintained my weight. I was never depressed or experienced mood swings. In fact, I felt great throughout my chemotherapy, which is a miracle in itself!

Additionally, I did not take an anti-cancer drug prescribed for me post-mastectomy, despite my oncologist's insistence that it was absolutely necessary given my cancer's high chances for recurrence within five years. Here it is almost 2019—nearly ten years after my initial diagnosis—and I've remained cancer-free and feeling great without having taken that drug!

I credit the Lord, first and foremost, for these and other miracles I experienced during my cancer journey. In the New Testament, there are numerous examples of Jesus' miraculous healings. As a strong Christian with an unshakable faith in the Lord and His Divine powers, I believed from the get-go that He *could* heal me. My encounter with Him on that Super Bowl Sunday confirmed that He *would* heal me. And He did.

I also acknowledge my expert Atlanta doctors in my story—particularly my oncologist, Dr. Perry Ballard. He was the one who initially informed me of the deadly nature of my disease, and the way he and Dr. Bill Barber, my surgeon, planned to treat it. Ironically, this is what convinced me that I couldn't rely on medical science alone for a cure. Thankfully, I believed that God could completely heal me.

You might already be skeptical of my story. Frankly, that is the very reason I have waited so long to tell it. Up until now, I've only shared it with a few friends and family members. I wanted to share it with others, but was afraid they wouldn't believe me or understand it—even Christian "believers." At best, I thought my story would be met with extreme skepticism and responses like "there has to be another explanation to this." At worse, I feared they'd think I was downright crazy. This fear is what kept me from what God was calling me to do, which was to share my testimony.

Over the past few years, I had several "believing" friends and family members tell me that I should publish my story, saying that it would give so much hope, inspiration and encouragement to those who are battling cancer or other potentially terminal diseases. A friend of mine, who happens to be a professional writer and the co-author of this book, added, "Lisa, you have to write down and share your experience with others. It will help so many people struggling with all kinds of disease to know that they have hope and healing with God. It could change their outcomes like it did yours."

Then God put it on my heart to do so, revealing to me

several times this verse from Habakkuk 2:2: "Write down the revelation and make it plain on tablets so that a herald can run with it." Those words resonated with me and told me that as a Christian, I had an obligation to help and encourage others with my testimony, no matter what my fears were about sharing it. Later, I had a revelation from God—discussed at the end of this book—which made me do just that.

Blessedly, my writer friend agreed to help me put my story to paper. Thankfully, Dr. Ballard also agreed to participate in my endeavor.

So here it is.

Foreword by
Dr. W. Perry Ballard, III

In March 2018, Lisa West *wrote to me about a book she hoped to write on her breast cancer experience. She wanted to know if I'd be willing to participate in that endeavor and be interviewed by a writer that she'd contracted for that purpose. Her letter went on to say that she felt my involvement would be crucial to her story.*

As her oncologist, I treated Lisa for Clinical Stage 3, Grade 3, locally advanced invasive ductal carcinoma of the left breast, initially diagnosed in late December of 2009.

I immediately wrote back "yes" to her request. I believed and told her that she had a remarkable story to tell as a breast cancer survivor, which would inspire and give hope to many who are struggling with this insidious disease.

Lisa's story was remarkable in many respects, most specifically in how she overcame huge odds in defeating her very large, rapidly growing and, in my professional opinion, potentially morbid tumor that initially seemed out of control. After only two rounds of chemo, I could no longer feel her previously rock-solid mass when supine, and only vaguely when sitting up. She also tolerated one of the most brutal chemo regimens out there without a hiccup. Additionally, her mastectomy pathology report amazingly revealed no cancer whatsoever in the surgically removed breast tissue (when usually some residual cancer is found). Lastly, she declined to take an anti-cancer drug (Arimidex) that I prescribed to prevent typical recurrence of her type of cancer within five years. Yet, she's remained cancer-free for nearly ten years after her initial diagnosis without taking this drug.

In my long experience as an oncologist, those examples of Lisa's case were truly miraculous. As a physician, I cannot explain those—or her apparent healing after only two rounds of chemo treatments—by medical science alone. I, of course, do believe that medical treatment played a part in her recovery. But I also believe that God played a major part in her ultimate healing.

In retrospect today, I believe that I, along with Lisa's surgeon, Dr. William Barber, were serving as agents or intermediaries of God in her treatment, healing and recovery.

Co-author/Editor Notes to Readers:

Dr. Ballard's comments throughout this book were taken from a recorded interview with him on May 2, 2018, as well as verbatim notes from his copious medical records on Lisa West from January 4, 2010 until May 23, 2012. In order to enhance the narrative flow as well as the reader's understanding of medical terms in the book, artistic license was taken in: paraphrasing Dr. Ballard's commentary and medical notes; placing that within the narrative of this book according to its chapter contents and sequencing; and expanding on certain information where clarification of medical terms and procedures was deemed necessary.

CHAPTER 1

In the Beginning

"And though your beginning was small,
your latter days will be very great."
– Job 8:7 (ESV)

I WASN'T ALWAYS A CHRISTIAN—that is, in the true sense of the word. That didn't happen until I was 40 years old, 13 years before I was diagnosed with cancer.

I grew up as a Methodist within a very loving, close-knit family. While my parents, sisters and I attended a church in our Atlanta neighborhood practically every Sunday during my childhood, that was about the extent of our Christian life. We never discussed religion, God or the Bible at home. In fact, even though we probably had a Bible in our home, I don't remember ever seeing one.

However, every night from my earliest memories, I'd say my prayers before going to bed. As simple and per-functory as those were, the ritual of reciting them was hugely comforting to me. I had gleaned from Sunday school that prayer time was when little ole me could have an audience with big magical God, who was supposedly concerned about my welfare and would provide me blessings. So I stuck with this nightly routine throughout my grade school years—eventually adding my own dialog to my memorized church verses. All the while, though, I still did not fully believe that God could hear my prayers or that He was even real.

I believe the reason I found my evening prayers so comforting is because I was born a very fearful and insecure child. Even though I had the best, most supportive parents in the world, three sweet sisters, a wonderful home and a great childhood overall, I was often plagued with anxiety and worry—usually over the most mundane or irrational things. Saying my prayers gave me the sense that some unseen, powerful being was watching over me.

When I was nine years old, my fears and anxiety worsened after watching an Alfred Hitchcock movie (*Vertigo*) that scared the living daylights out of me. After that, I began to be fearful about going to sleep at night as soon as it got dark outside. I started having regular panic attacks before going to bed, though I didn't know then that's what they were or were called. I was too embarrassed to tell anyone about all of this, including my parents, because I thought they'd think I was crazy. Around this time, I also began to mildly stutter. Still not fully believing that God was real, I didn't know that I could call on Him to help me with and heal these afflictions. Consequently, I would suffer with both for decades.

My speech impediment grew exponentially worse in seventh grade at Tuxedo Elementary School, when a former best and hugely popular friend turned the whole grade against me. As a result, I was relentlessly bullied that entire school year, and had only one friend. Once again, I was too embarrassed to tell my parents about this. When my parents eventually caught on to what was happening, they wanted to intervene. I persuaded them not to for fear of even worse reprisals.

What sustained me through that horrible year were the constant love, support and friendship of my mom and dad. Looking back on that today, I realize how blessed I was to have them for parents. Their love mirrored God's: it was unconditional and unwavering. And, it gave me the foundation for having a steadfast trust and faith in a much higher parental being—a.k.a., my Heavenly Father —much later in my life.

Another important person who also helped me through that terrible year was my teacher. When bullying began on the playground, she'd always call me to come inside. I'll never forget the time she drove me home from school one day just before summer break. On the way home, she stopped by Dykes High School (where I'd start eighth grade in the fall) to pick up her daughter. While waiting for her, my teacher said to me, "Lisa, this will be your school for the next five years. It will give you a whole new beginning. There will be students from three other elementary schools besides Tuxedo in your classes. They won't have known you or your past, so you'll be able to start over with lots of new friends. You're a very cute and sweet girl, *and I **know** that you will be popular.*"

I had dreaded going to Dykes until my teacher spoke those words. They gave me a glimmer of hope that things might turnaround for me in high school. Those words turned out to be prophetic. Looking back on that today, I believe that God used my teacher to speak them into being, because what she said actually came true.

When I entered high school, I immediately had tons of friends and was popular with girls and guys alike. Meanwhile, I'd become a master at hiding my stuttering— and my panic attacks only happened at night in privacy. Aside from saying my nightly prayers, occasionally going to church with my family, and attending a few Young Life meetings, God remained in the periphery of my life throughout my wonderful high school years.

That trend continued during my college years at the University of South Carolina. My life was going great. The only real difficulty I had was in completing my class assignments and making passing grades! Schoolwork had never been easy for me. In fact, I probably would have been diagnosed with Attention Deficit Disorder (ADD) as a child if that diagnosis existed back then. Good thing my parents didn't care about academic performance!

The summer before my senior year, I met the love of my life on a blind date! After five years of dating, Vincent West and I were married on May 23, 1981, at Trinity Presbyterian Church. We moved into a large ranch house in the Buckhead area of Atlanta, and started a family. Within five years of our marriage, we had three children: Ansley, born in 1983; Lindsay (called Cubby), born in 1985; and Vincent, Jr., born in 1988.

Outwardly, I enjoyed a privileged life. I had three precious young children, a beautiful home, and a wonderful husband who provided us with a great lifestyle. I had a housekeeper twice a week to help me with house chores and the kids. I played on a tennis team, and enjoyed being a volunteer at my kids' schools. I'd also found a passion for flower arranging and decorating, and was hired and paid for doing flower arrangements for private parties. In fact, I handled Christmas decorations for a major Atlanta hotel for two consecutive years. I was hugely fulfilled by all of these activities—as well as being a stay-at-home, hands-on mom, just like mine had been.

Yet with all my happiness as a mother, party planner, decorator, and Vincent's wife, I was still plagued with evening panic attacks, which had worsened with Vincent's constant business traveling. I was afraid to stay at home on nights when he was gone—even though we had a high-tech alarm system. Amazingly, I usually got a friend or family member to do things with me and the kids those evenings, and to spend the night with us (or at least stay until I got the kids to bed and knew that the house was secure). That was the only way I could fall asleep.

During these early married and motherhood years, I also became riddled with constant anxiety and worry due to my self-imposed pressures to be a great wife and mother and to have a beautiful home. I additionally struggled with my self-esteem and confidence due to my (again, self-imposed) need to have Vincent's approval on everything, even though he never put pressure on me about anything. As a result of that and my ADD nature, I often felt inadequate and overwhelmed. I'd fret and obsess over the most mundane things—daily asking my best friend if I should worry about this or that (she always said "no!").

And, I was still a "closet" stutterer.

Basically, and unbeknownst to no one, I had reverted to the same highly anxious person that I was in elementary school. I had no control over the fears that caused my incessant worry and panic attacks. Nor did I have a spiritual connection with God to help relieve me of those. While Vincent and I were members of Trinity Presbyterian Church, we were secular Christians at best, just like my family growing up. We went to church on Sundays and our kids attended Sunday school—but that was about it.

It would be nearly a decade later before God truly

came into my life. And when He did, it would be a life-changing experience that ultimately healed all of these afflictions.

FEAR NOT!

CHAPTER 2

An Oasis in the Wilderness

*"Forget the former things; do not dwell
on the past. See, I am doing a new thing!
Now it springs up; do you not perceive it?
I am making a way in the wilderness and
streams in the wasteland."*
– Isaiah 43:18-19 (NIV)

IN 1992, WHEN I WAS 36 years old (and the kids were nine, seven and four years old respectively), we hired a new housekeeper, Mary Office, who worked for us three days a week. Vincent was still working long hours and traveling constantly for his family's lumber business. Understandably, he didn't have time to help with the ever-increasing household chores, after-school activities and driving that three children entailed.

I didn't know then what a Godsend Mary would turn out to literally be—not just in her housekeeping and childcare capabilities, but also in her amazing Christian faith and spiritual gifts that would ultimately change my life. In retrospect today, I know that God brought Mary into my life because He knew that I was struggling and needed a mentor like her to bring me to faith in Him.

17

From the start, I sensed that Mary was very religious, and she rightly sensed that I wasn't interested in any of that. Having worked for similar employers, she knew what a turn-off sharing her faith and beliefs could be to them. So, she mentioned her beliefs only in rare situations that allowed her to subtly do so, without being pushy or overbearing in any way.

During the first two years of Mary's employment, I hardly gave her the time of day—leaving her a list of chores and dashing out the door practically the minute she arrived. I did notice, however, that she always had a smile on her face. In fact, her whole being radiated peace and joy. She never complained or copped an attitude, no matter what tasks I assigned her.

Mary began working full-time for us in 1994. In order to do that, she had to stop working for my sister Louise, who had long employed Mary twice a week. Louise was the one who had initially referred Mary to us for the days she wasn't working for her. I truly felt bad about this dilemma, so I asked Mary to pray about it and then make her own decision.

Mary ultimately chose to work for our family full-time. Her decision wasn't based on better pay, fewer tasks, or an easier workload. Nor was it based on favoritism (she would have definitely chosen Louise!). It was simply because the Lord clearly told Mary to "Go work for Lisa." So, she obeyed God and chose our family.

I was 38 at the time, and still inwardly struggling with anxiety and worry. Additionally, I'd started having constant stinging in my right eye—particularly at night, which led to horrible insomnia and, in turn, more stinging in my eye during the day. After seeing a string of doctors over many months, one finally put me on Prozac, a relatively new anti-anxiety and anti-depression drug. Right away, this drug solved my eye problems!

I also saw a psychiatrist about my insomnia. He flat out told me, "You don't have insomnia; you are having panic attacks because you are afraid of going to sleep!" That's when I first heard the term "panic attack" to describe my decades-long "secret" affliction, and learned that it was a bona fide medical condition suffered by many! What a relief it was to know this!

While dealing with these health issues over that year, Mary's happy demeanor began to intrigue me even more. So, on one of my particularly "down" days, I finally asked her why she was always so cheerful and never appeared to have any problems.

Mary told me that she struggled with lots of problems. Her husband had left her 16 years ago for another woman, leaving her to raise their four children on her own. Her two rebellious teenage boys were constantly in trouble at school or with the law. She had to make arrangements for her younger daughters when she stayed with my kids at night and on weekends. And, she was just scraping by financially, barely making ends meet.

"Wow!" I thought. All of this was a real eye-opener to my self-absorbed self! "So how can you be so happy in spite of all that?" I asked her.

She went on to tell me about her strong Christian faith in Jesus and how she turned all of her problems over to Him. Her faith was more than just hoping God would turn difficult circumstances around for the better and help her through them; it was trusting, believing and knowing with 100 percent certainty that He would. He'd proven that to her with one miracle after another throughout her life, and had always delivered on His promises to her. Her faith is what allowed her to face and overcome the toughest of obstacles with a smile on her face.

I couldn't relate at all to what she was telling me. Yes, I was a "Christian"—but I knew virtually nothing about Jesus or having that kind of belief, trust and faith in Him. For that matter, I hardly knew what Christianity was about or encompassed—outside of obeying the Ten Commandments and attending church on Sundays.

Mary told me she was a member of a Pentecostal Church, and that its fellowship also supported her through hard times. In a matter of words, she said Pentecostals believe in the literal interpretation of the Bible, including the Old Testament. As such, they observe the Jewish Sabbath and Jewish dietary (kosher) laws. But most importantly, they seek a direct personal experience of God through Baptism with the Holy Spirit, which enables them to live a Spirit-filled and empowered life. This empowerment includes spiritual gifts, such as speaking in tongues and divine healing.

All of this sounded like Holy-rolling, fire-and-brim-stone, and evangelical fundamentalism to me! As you might imagine, it was way outside of my Presbyterian comfort zone. While I desperately wanted Mary's worry-free happiness, I was still unsure about my own Christian beliefs and faith—and definitely wasn't ready to embrace hers!

It was then 1995, and I was 39 years old. Around this time, I told Mary that I wanted to get off the Prozac I'd been taking for about a year. While it had cured my eye problem, it also made me extremely tired and lethargic. I was normally a very high-energy person and I hated this side effect of the drug. Mary said to me, "Lisa, we can pray to the Lord about this until you feel comfortable giving this problem to Him. But I know that when you do, He will take care of it."

So, I stopped taking the Prozac cold turkey, and prayed daily with Mary about that. Within a week, my eye problem miraculously disappeared and never resurfaced. Plus, I never experienced any drug-withdrawal side effects! Even by medical standards, the latter was a miracle. It's recommended that you get off such anti-anxiety drugs by tapering off the dosage over a two- to three-week period.

I also then started praying about my panic attacks. Initially during my prayer mission to heal this ailment, I would freeze with fear when an attack surfaced. I would immediately start praying to the Lord, giving this ailment over to Him, and reciting certain Biblical verses repeatedly. Of all those, the one that I'd always repeat is from 1 John 4:4, which reads: "He that is in me is greater than he that is in the world."

In this verse, the "He that is in me" refers to God, who dwells within me (as well as all believers) through His Holy Spirit. God "is greater" and more powerful than the enemy, the "he that is in the world," who'd kept me in fear of having panic attacks. By reciting this verse routinely and repeatedly over the next couple of months when an attack would pop up, I gradually became less fearful of them. Eventually, I got to where I trusted totally in the Lord, knowing He would take care of the attacks and my fear of them.

It would take roughly five months for God to eradicate my panic attacks—much longer than the week it took to heal my eye problem without Prozac. But like the latter, once I was healed, I never suffered a panic attack again! After more than twenty years without them, I hardly remember having them!

Amazed and galvanized by these two back-to-back Divine healing experiences, I eagerly wanted to know more (and more) about Mary's Jesus—who seemingly helped her with everything, including healings—but who also gave her so much peace and joy. And that's when the door opened to my real journey into Christianity.

FEAR NOT!

CHAPTER 3

My Journey Begins: From Baby Steps to Born Again

> *"Blessed be the God and Father of our Lord Jesus Christ, who according to His great mercy has caused us to be born again to a living hope through the resurrection of Jesus Christ from the dead."*
> – 1 Peter 1:3 (NASB)

MY TRUE CHRISTIAN JOURNEY began with tiny baby steps. Over the remainder of 1995 and into 1996, I questioned Mary about all kinds of things related to Jesus, Scripture and prayer, as well as her testimony on how she came to be a born-again believer. All the while, I kept my distance, as I was not yet ready to make a giant leap into Christianity.

Mary's testimony was mind-blowing! She grew up in a very religious, dirt-poor farm family of eleven children that couldn't afford medical care and often enough food. They prayed fervently and constantly to the Lord, who answered their prayers with one miracle after another, including Divine healings of all sorts of sickness and illnesses. Witnessing those miracles and answered prayers built Mary's faith and dependence on the Lord.

Mary was baptized as a born-again Christian at the age of 18. Times were hard when her husband left her just after that, but God always provided for her and her family. She hadn't divorced her husband after all these years because she still loved him, and the Lord had told her that He would bring him back to her. (That actually happened in July of 2005, and they've been together ever since!)

I began sharing my worries and concerns with Mary on a regular basis. She could immediately direct me to Bible verses, stories and testimonies that would uncannily address those, as she knew the Bible inside and out.

God spoke to me through these Bible passages—particularly the stories and testimonies filled with miracles. God drew me to Him through these vehicles. Reading every one of these passages brought me so much comfort, peace and hope. I began to grab hold of certain testimonies and stories in the Bible that related to my own life and experiences, and in which I clearly heard God speak to me through His words.

This is when I began to fully believe in God's miraculous powers and miracles. I started believing that if God could perform miracles in the Bible, then these miracles would be available to me, too. I wanted them all, and I went after them as best I could.

Beyond this, I didn't need any further evidence to know if God or Jesus Christ were real in order to believe in Him. I simply believed and had faith in Him based on Scripture. Unlike me, others I knew couldn't embrace Christianity and belief in Christ until they had hard, historical evidence or sound, theological essays on Jesus' life, ministry, miracles and resurrection. Only when they had proven evidence of that—from books like Lee Strobel's *The Case for Christ* or *Mere Christianity* by C. S. Lewis—could they make a leap of faith into Christianity.

All of that said, I *still* didn't know how Christian I wanted to be.

The more I studied the Bible, the more I realized the importance of setting aside an hour of quiet time daily to be with the Lord in prayer and study of Scripture. I knew that's how I would start to have a personal relationship with Him. I also knew that I needed to learn how to hear God's answers to my prayers. Initially, I didn't do so great with my daily devotional hour. I didn't quite know what to say to God or how to pray to Him, so I usually gave my "quiet time" lip service and cut it way short of an hour. This wasn't yet a priority in my life—so I'd often blow it off if my schedule couldn't fully accommodate it.

Honestly, even though I was absorbing like a sponge

everything Mary was teaching me, I was still unsure about where I stood in my faith—or how that would fit into my everyday life. I only had my big toe in the water, so to speak. I definitely wasn't ready to embrace Mary's Pentecostal faith; that was too over-the-top and all-encompassing for my privileged world. So I continued to compartmentalize my Christianity: pulling it out and paying attention to it when I needed it; and ignoring it when inconvenient.

But God was determined to get my full attention. He did exactly that through not only Mary, but also through certain people whose Christianity more mirrored my upbringing and comfort level. One was Pam Elting, the mother of one of Ansley's friends, who I'd just met. Pam was openly a very strong believer, but she seemed so "normal" in spite of that. Another was my sister-in-law, Margie Wynne, who'd just become a true believer. That year, they both invited me to join their respective Bible Study groups. While they had both made a positive impression on me, I declined their invitations because I was still too unsure about my faith to participate in them.

Then, at the age of 40, I made a major turn in my faith by becoming a born-again Christian at a Christian couples retreat that was organized by Pam, held at our Ellijay farm, and led by two well-known Atlanta ministers. On the second day of the retreat, I publicly declared my belief and faith in Jesus Christ as my personal Savior and Lord, surrendering my life to Him and trusting in all He did for me through the cross: that His blood cleansed all of my sins; that He paid the penalty of death for all of mankind's sins, thus providing all believers with the free gift of eternal life; that He was buried; and that He was resurrected on the third day (and appeared to more than 500 eyewitnesses).

In believing this, I was born again by the Spirit of God as a new creation—and I immediately wanted to be baptized. The ministers at the retreat performed my Baptism right then and there. I was elated!

Though I'd been moving towards salvation and baptism as public identification of my relationship with Christ—and as a first step of obedience to Him, I hadn't planned for that to happen at this retreat. But I felt a strong calling from God to do so.

I came home ecstatic by my Baptism, which I immediately shared with my family members and friends. Understandably, they didn't get my seemingly overnight, newfound Christianity. Nor did they appreciate my overboard zealousness and self-righteousness in spouting off about it. Looking back on that now, I can see why I turned them off. In all of my excitement about being a true Christian, I initially did not act like one.

After my Baptism, I started attending Pam's Bible study at Peachtree Presbyterian Church (PPC) and soon became in charge of hospitality. A couple of years after that, another friend invited me to attend a women's Bible study on the subject of faith at Northside United Methodist Church (NUMC). The richness of that study and its smaller size was more akin to what I was seeking, so I became a regular member of it and left PPC.

Just before my second year at NUMC, the head of its Women's Bible Study called to ask if I would be willing to lead a small group of Bible Study participants. I politely turned her down, without telling her that it was because of my lack of confidence in being a leader and public speaker. An hour later she called me back, saying that she'd clearly heard from the Lord that He wanted me to be a leader. I was overwhelmed and shocked by that!

I didn't want to say "no" to her or the Lord, and be disobedient to Him. But I just couldn't imagine myself in this position! So I told her that I would think about it and get back to her.

I realized that my fear of leading and speaking before a group was keeping me from accepting this position— and from fulfilling my potential as a believer in service to the Lord. Fear is not of God; it is the enemy that keeps you from growing in the Lord.

I then remembered the story of Moses, the humblest of men in the eyes of the Lord, who was called by God to lead the Israelites out of bondage in Egypt. In a matter of words, Moses thought he wasn't up to this task for several reasons. He argued with God over these, telling Him that he thought the elders of Israel wouldn't believe God had appeared to and asked him to do this great thing. He also told God that he feared that the Egyptians wouldn't listen to his pleas on behalf of His people. On top of that, he said that he was not eloquent, and was slow of speech and tongue. He finally said to God, "Pardon your servant, Lord. Please send someone else." (Exodus 4:13, NIV)

But God would not take "no" for an answer from Moses. For every one of Moses' voiced fears and reservations, God Himself provided him with solutions—including using Aaron, his well-spoken brother, as his mouthpiece when speaking to the Israelites. Plus, God would tell both of them what to say to the Egyptians—and teach Moses what to do. Basically, God told Moses He would have his back. The rest of the story, as they say, is history.

What's amazing about this story is its dual messages about God's ability to free us from the things that bind us in a cocoon of fear: (1) through faith in God, Moses was able to lead His people out of Egyptian slavery and into the Promised Land; and (2) through faith in God, Moses was able to be victorious over his weaknesses and be freed from his fears about those. As most everybody knows, Moses became a legendary leader, and the greatest of prophets in the Old Testament.

I am in no way trying to compare myself to Moses, but his story resonated with me. If Moses could lead two million Jews out of Egyptian slavery in spite of his speech impediment and self-esteem issues, I could certainly try to lead a small Bible study group—especially knowing that God would help and be with me.

I had roughly 20 women in my group that year. I was still petrified about leading and speaking in front of them. I thought I was a horrible leader—but my group members thought otherwise. Everyone was so nice, complimentary and participatory throughout the study. From that experience, I gained confidence in my leadership abilities as well as self-esteem—plus overcame my fear of public speaking—praise be to our awesome God! Buoyed by this, I agreed to be a group leader the next year.

Looking back on that now, I see how this experience was a pivotal one in my life. God wanted to show me that through Christ, I could do anything—including becoming an effective leader who was free from past insecurities, fears and worries. It's amazing to me that our Heavenly Father knows exactly how to change our lives for the better through certain people and situations!

My newfound self-esteem and confidence from that experience extended to other aspects of my life as well. I no longer had to depend on other people for assurances, validations or compliments. I now had God's affirmations!

This changed me for the better and, in the process, the dynamics and success of my marriage as well.

From this and other experiences in my faith journey, I finally got it that God truly loved me unconditionally for the unique person He made me to be—even with all my human flaws and foibles. Just knowing this is self-affirming! I also realized that God gave me certain gifts that I could use towards His Glory.

One of those is the gift of faith—that is, the ability to believe in the unseen promises of God, and to impart that to others. The other skill God gave me is the ability to fully listen, understand and respond to fellow believers having personal issues or problems, using God's Word to help them with those. I've never been book-smart, but I've always been interested in people, their relationships, their stories and their testimonies. Using these gifts for God's glory gave me a sense of purpose in my faith journey.

Through my participation at both PPC and NUMC, I found my niche with a whole new group of Christian friends who were seeking a deeper, more intimate relationship with God like I was. Then, in 1997, another friend took my Christian journey several steps further by inviting me to a Sunday service at North Point Community Church (NP) in Alpharetta, recently founded and led by the gifted pastor Andy Stanley.

This non-denominational church was right up my alley. Its mission was simply "to lead people into a growing relationship with Jesus Christ." Andy's messages were powerful in their practical applicability to everyday life. Unlike past church experiences I had, I always left his services feeling uplifted and unconditionally loved by God—just like I wanted to feel after attending church. I loved the whole experience and started attending NP regularly.

Vincent and I also attended a couples' retreat led by Andy on the subject of marriage, which was equally awesome. Through these experiences, I decided that I wanted God to be front and center in all aspects of my life.

As time went on, the Holy Spirit began to convict me of other things in my life, which I knew were wrong and that I knew He wanted to purify me of (things like jealousy, envy, gossip, etc.).

I began to seriously commit an hour each morning to be with the Lord. I would read and study the Bible, praise the Lord in worship, and pray to Him—pouring out my heart and desires out to Him, while also asking Him for guidance and help with my concerns as well as those of others. This daily devotional gave me so much peace and comfort that it quickly became a priority and treasured part of my day. It still is.

Through my church attendance, Bible studies, personal time in the Word (Scripture), and, of course, prayer time with Mary, I also was learning how to develop my spiritual faculties so that I could hear and discern God's voice, guidance and answers to my prayers. One way to hear Him is through God's "still, quiet voice" that speaks to us in our minds. It also could be through a moment of sudden intuition, or an unmistakable "sign in the road," so to speak, in answer to prayer. Another way to discern God's guidance is through the wisdom and counsel of godly mentors and fellow believing friends. And, it could be through visions and dreams, which is the first and most prevalent way I would hear God speak to me.

My first experience of that was during the aforementioned couples retreat. On the second night of that, I had a fully awake vision—that is, not while sleeping. It was of a fierce battle scene between two opposing sides at war. Just after the retreat, I experienced another God-sent message. While showering, I heard a voice in my head that repeatedly uttered one word: Job. Not job like a work job, but Job from the Old Testament.

I asked Mary about these back-to-back revelations, as they were. She told me that God was trying to warn me that I would be facing real-life battles of my own, and that I needed to have the faith and "the patience of Job" to get through those.

I immediately devoured the "Book of Job." In a nutshell for those unfamiliar with this book, Job was considered a servant of God like no one else on earth: blameless, upright, fearing God, and turning away from evil. Satan comes to God and basically says to Him, "Job's faith is not based on his love for God, but only on his good fortune and desire for rewards; take away Job's good fortune and he will curse God." God thus allows Satan to test Job's faith by bringing great loss, sorrow and suffering into his life. Job doesn't understand his inexplicable suffering or why God has allowed it (his friends say he must have sinned). Yet through it all, he never curses God or loses his faith in Him.

Towards the end of his suffering, Job asks God why He allowed his profound suffering. God's response to him reveals His infinite power, wonders and sovereignty. He tells Job that finite humans can't begin to understand how He rules the universe, why He allows suffering, or why circumstances aren't to our liking. As the Bible tells us, "His ways are higher than our ways, and His thoughts are higher than our thoughts" (Isaiah 55: 8-9, NASB).

In the end, after all of Job's suffering, God restores his fortunes and increases all that he had twofold. "The LORD blessed the latter days of Job more than his beginning" (Job 42:12, NASB).

The bottom-line takeaway from this story is that we must always—no matter the circumstances—trust, obey and have faith in God. As our Almighty Creator, we must believe that He loves us, and that He always has our best interests at heart.

I'll admit, I didn't understand the relevance of this book for me at the time. I couldn't identify with Job, because everything was going great in my life—with my marriage, my children and my friends. But Mary was right: God's revelation of Job to me was prophetic. I would soon experience one trial after another—including one that would test my faith to its outermost limits.

CHAPTER 4

Mary, My Mentor

"Your statutes are my delight; they are my counselors."
— Psalm 119:24 (NIV)

"All Scripture is God-breathed and is useful for teaching, rebuking, correcting and training in righteousness, so that the servant of God may be thoroughly equipped for every good work."
— 2 Timothy 3:16-17 (NIV)

WHEN LISA ASKED ME to work full-time for her, I told her she'd be "stealing" me from her sister, Louise, who I worked for two days a week. So like I always do, I prayed about it and I heard the Lord say go work for Lisa. Even though God wanted me to go to Lisa, Louise truly treated me better. She was much nicer and friendlier than Lisa, who was standoffish and always running in and out of the door.

But I obeyed God and went to work for Lisa. "So what do you want me to do in this (Lisa's) home?" I asked the Lord. He revealed to me that Lisa was carrying a gift that He wanted to bring out and use for His glory.

Like I said, Lisa hardly paid me attention when I first went to work for her. It wasn't until I was working full-time for her that she started asking me questions about my faith. And when that happened, she opened the door for me to tell her about Jesus. I had wanted to share things about Him before, but I knew she wasn't ready for that then. It probably would have scared her off.

When Lisa was ready to learn about Jesus, I'd never seen anyone so hungry and eager to know about Him. The more I shared with her my experiences of His powers and miracles, the more she wanted to know about Him. Sometimes people accept what you tell them, but most times they don't. Lisa accepted God's word with such excitement that we soon began praying regularly together about things in her life.

I then knew why God told me to go work for Lisa, versus Louise, even though I hadn't wanted to. Lisa needed God, and I was able to lead her to Him. It was all part of His plan. God works in mysterious ways, according to His perfect timing. We don't always know why God calls us to do something or why things are going badly. But if we remain prayerful and obedient to Him, He will eventually reveal the why, which in my experience, always turns out for the better. That's why I always say to wait patiently on the Lord.

So when Lisa asked me about my life and how I came to give it to Jesus, I gradually shared my testimony with her. When she came to me with problems or concerns, I directed her to Scripture about those. She wanted to learn how to pray and how to discern the Lord's voice in answer to her prayers, so I helped her with that, too. Eventually, she was able to hear Him loud and clear, mostly through dreams. This strengthened her faith and helped her get through trials that would come into her life. There would be many of those, several of which would test her faith. But God helped her through all of those in a mighty way.

CHAPTER 5

Trials and Tribulations

> *"Finally, be strong in the Lord and in His mighty power. Put on the full armor of God, so that you can take your stand against the devil's schemes. For our struggle is not against flesh and blood, but against the rulers, against the authorities, against the powers of this dark world and against the spiritual forces of evil in the heavenly realms."*
>
> – **Ephesians 6:10-12 (NIV)**

MARY HAD BEEN RIGHT in her interpretation of the prophetic signs revealed to me in the Book of Job. The next ten or so years of my life following my Baptism—from my early 40s into my early 50s—would, indeed, bring many trials and tribulations that would test my faith repeatedly.

My daughters were now in their teenage years. Like any other mother with children in that peer-pressure phase of life, I was faced with new parenting challenges to keep them on the right, straight and narrow track. All in all, my girls were great kids who excelled academically and socially (and who, today, are successful adults in terms of their careers and own families). That said, there were many occasions when I had to pull in the reigns on their testing of limits and independence.

My son was now in middle school, which is when many boys start "to push the envelope," so to speak, as a rite of passage into high school, when they push the envelope even further! So I had to stay on top of him, too, with regards to his schoolwork, friends he was hanging out with, afterschool activities and weekend plans.

Having been diagnosed with auditory processing problems in the first grade, Vincent, Jr., spent grades two through four at a private school for children with learning disabilities. During his first year there, he was diagnosed with Attention Deficit Disorder (ADD), the symptoms of which include the inability to focus and concentrate. His teachers wanted him to be on Adderall, a drug used to treat children with ADD, because they believed it would help him with his studies and schoolwork. They told Vincent and me that many children at the school took such prescribed medication, and that it hugely helped them to focus on and complete their schoolwork.

These diagnoses weren't around when I grew up. If they had been, and as I said before, I probably would have been diagnosed as ADD or ADHD myself. But because these syndromes and medications to treat them didn't exist in my early school years, I had to learn how to buckle down, concentrate and do my schoolwork without medication. This resolve came primarily from my teachers' strict discipline that applied to me as well as to other kids who couldn't focus or sit still. I didn't make the greatest of grades in my classes, but I always passed them.

So . . . I wondered if these diagnoses could sometimes be misdiagnoses that labeled normal children who have lots of energy (and thus, the inability to focus) with a learning disability. I don't like labels of any kind when it comes to kids, because they often cause a self-fulfilling prophecy. For example: a student labeled as ADD or ADHD believes that he/she has a bona fide learning disability, and thus believes that he/she can only be successful in school by taking "x" drug. The student then comes to rely on that drug (versus their own abilities and resourcefulness) as a mental, emotional and often social crutch.

I also considered that Adderall was a relatively new drug for treating kids with ADD and ADHD. There were no studies on the effects of its long-term use. In fact, after meeting with Vincent, Jr.'s teachers about his ADD, I remember Vincent saying to me, "You know that our son will be a guinea pig for this drug. We have no idea of how it will ultimately affect him."

At the same time, Vincent and I knew lots of people whose children were on Adderall. Their kids were doing great in school as a result. Given all of these opposing viewpoints about the drug, we were truly conflicted about Vincent, Jr., being on it.

All of that said, and after much discussion, trepidation and reluctance, Vincent and I finally agreed with Vincent, Jr.'s teachers to put him on Adderall. We then felt we were making the best decision based on the facts at hand. In retrospect, we wish we had never made that decision.

Today, Adderall is one of the most over-prescribed, addictive and abused drugs on the market. It is treated like a Class II (controlled substance) drug and requires a written prescription presented to a pharmacy in person to have it filled. And because this drug provides an amphetamine-like high when abused, it often leads to interest, experimentation and use of other likewise upper drugs, as well as downers. Of course, Vincent and I didn't know any of this about the drug when we had to make a decision about Vincent, Jr., being on it.

Again, I know and understand that his drug has helped many children with learning issues. In my son's case, however, it was the wrong drug for him to be on. Additionally, through certain doctors, it became way overprescribed for him.

Meanwhile during this decade of my life, Vincent undertook the task of closing down his family-owned business. This was stressful for our family in terms of lifestyle changes we had to make. Until Vincent was able to start a new business, we had to tighten our belts on spending. Most distressing to me regarding this were two things. First, I had to cut back on Mary's employment from full-time to two days a week. I didn't mind the loss of her daily housekeeping help, but I would sorely miss the everyday spiritual mentoring, guidance and sustenance that she always provided me.

Secondly, we had to put the family farm in Ellijay on the market, which was very sad for all of my family. Vincent and I, along with our kids, cherished this place. We had spent nearly every weekend there since we bought it in 1991. It held so many memories of great times for all of us.

(Fast forward: Thanks to Vincent's business acumen, we were not only able to hold onto the farm, but also to develop part of it into a successful mountain-home community. Vincent also started a new business that was enormously successful. Under his helm, it grew to be a national retailing giant, as well as a publicly traded company on the New York Stock Exchange.)

Then, in 2009, I was diagnosed with Graves' disease, an autoimmune disorder that causes overactivity of the thyroid gland, or hyperthyroidism. If not managed and controlled, this disease can result in death.

Before I was diagnosed with Graves' disease, I had exhibited several of its symptoms—namely, unexplained weight loss, nervousness, excitability and irregular heart beat. However, I had none of the disease's typical and main causes: genetics and environmental factors. But I did have a lesser cause: severe emotional stress. Though my endocrinologist put me on medication to control and manage the disease, I was still freaked out that I had even contracted it.

Several things sustained me through all of these trials. One was my daily devotional time with the Lord in prayer, worship and study. I found myself drawn to Scriptures that addressed whatever I was praying for. I would devour these verses and ponder on them for days, until God gave me a sense of peace that He would handle my problems and requests.

At the same time, I surrounded myself with Christianity in all of its aspects that dealt with my life and illness. This included listening to Christian radio stations, and attending many church programs featuring miraculous testimonies of individuals who had overcome major life obstacles, including serious diseases, through belief and faith in God.

Another source of spiritual sustenance was a weekly prayer group formed in my early 40s. It comprised five women who wanted to pray regularly for our children and the issues that we faced. Prayer in numbers is always more powerful than individual prayer, and this turned out to be a great support group for all of us.

Additionally, there was the constant support and spiritual guidance of Mary. Even though she was now only in my home two days a week, she was always available to pray with me over the phone about anything that I felt the need to pray for.

Finally and most importantly was the constant support, love and backing of my wonderful husband. Vincent and I have always been a team when it comes to our children and decisions about them. We encourage each other to never give up—despite what they might be facing—knowing that there is always a hopeful solution. That is what hope in the Lord ultimately is: belief that He will turn around situations for the better.

Through the trials we faced during these years with our children, Vincent's business and my Graves' disease, our marriage and love for each other only grew stronger.

Without Vincent, I couldn't have gotten through any of these trials—or the ultimate one that I would soon face.

CHAPTER 6

Finding the Enemy

> *"But those who hope in the LORD will renew their strength. They will soar on wings like eagles; they will run and not grow weary, they will walk and not be faint."*
>
> **– Isaiah 40:31 (NIV)**

IN EARLY DECEMBER, while undressing one morning, I noticed a big blue vein running across my left breast. That's weird, I thought; maybe it's always been there but I'm just now seeing it. I wasn't concerned and ignored it, as I had no family history of breast cancer and had mammograms every year. The only abnormality ever reported was a suspicious spot in my right breast in July 2008. I had a follow-up mammogram of that breast six months after that, and it was negative.

But while showering one evening roughly two weeks after seeing that weird vein, I felt a rock hard place—about the size of a large Snickers bar—in my left breast. When I got out of the shower, I stared at my breasts in the mirror and again saw that large blue vein.

The first thing that goes through your mind when you feel something that foreign in your body is cancer. I was immediately overcome with fear and dread that it might be that. Vincent was out of town on business, so I called him to voice my concerns. He said, "I'm sure it's probably nothing—but call your doctor in the morning."

Then I called Mary. It was very late but, as always, she was available to pray with me about it.

Later that night in bed, I cried out to the Lord in prayer, saying "God, please don't let this be cancer! I already have Graves' disease! And my husband is constantly traveling to start a new business! I can't handle another crisis now—especially if it's cancer! You have to help me!"

I continued to argue with God for hours into the night. Eventually, the healing experiences I had heard from other peoples' testimonies, read in the Bible, and experienced in my own right bubbled up in my subconscious. I knew that God was telling me He would be with me and heal me. An awesome peace and assurance that I was going to be okay overcame me, and I was able to fall asleep. I'm certain that God gave me that peace.

The next morning (December 15), I called and explained my findings to my internist. Because it was the end of the year (when people with satisfied health-insurance deductibles for the calendar year schedule last-minute doctors appointments that will be covered by their insurance), she wasn't able to see me for a mammogram until early January. I told her that I absolutely couldn't wait that long! So, she ordered a bilateral mammogram and left-breast ultrasound for me at the Piedmont Breast Center that I could schedule on my own right away. However, I wasn't able to get an appointment until December 23— over a week away. It seemed like an eternity until then.

The medical technician who performed the mammogram and ultrasound was very serious and quiet throughout both procedures. Afterwards, she assigned me to a very sweet administrative nurse who said the tests revealed a new (that is, compared to my prior mammograms) solid mass in my left breast, measuring 3.2 centimeters (cm) at its largest dimension. She told me that she was immediately scheduling a biopsy of the mass. It was obvious to me that she and the technician both thought that I had cancer.

Given the Christmas holidays, the earliest available appointment for my biopsy was December 29, six long days away and another eternity of waiting. My daughter, Cubby, happened to be home for the holidays, so she went with me to my appointment. The technician who performed the biopsy confirmed what I thought, saying, "This should not be in your body! If it's not cancer, I still want it out!" It wasn't within his job parameters to voice his opinion on what he saw; that was solely the radiologist's job. The fact that he freely did so indicated to me that he was truly alarmed and concerned about the size of my tumorous mass.

Because of the holidays, my official biopsy report wouldn't be back until after the New Year. Once again, another eternity of waiting.

On the morning of December 31 (New Year's Eve), I got an unexpected phone call from Piedmont Breast Center. I wasn't supposed to hear back from them until after January 1. On the line was the sweet nurse who had ordered my biopsy. "Mrs. West," she began, "we've received the initial report from your biopsy. I am so sorry to tell you this, but it confirms that you have breast cancer."

Even though I had prepared myself for those words, it still was so strange—even surreal—to actually hear them.

"We are still waiting for the final results of your biopsy," she continued, "but the initial report shows that you have invasive ductal carcinoma in your left breast, which is the most common type of breast cancer. However, yours is estimated to be Grade 3, which means your cancer is fast growing and likely to spread." There was then silence on the phone, as I was too overwhelmed to say anything back.

She then told me that she'd already scheduled two appointments for me on Monday, January 4, with two Piedmont Hospital specialists. One was with Dr. William

Barber, one of Atlanta's top general surgeons who specializes in breast cancer surgery; the other was with Dr. Perry Ballard, a nationally renowned oncologist.

Vincent, of course, was devastated. At the time, we were at our farm in Ellijay, with plans to spend New Year's Eve there with several couples. Needless to say, we didn't feel like celebrating and cut the evening short. We didn't mention my news to anyone that day besides Mary, my girls and a close friend. Both Ansley and Cubby—who were then living in New Mexico and New York respectively—made plans to fly home in order to be with me during my appointments the coming week.

Naturally, I was scared. I'm human after all. But in my heart, I knew that I was going to be okay. God had given me His assurance, as well as a sense of peace, the night I found my tumor. Plus, I had a solid foundation and trust in His healing powers from what I had experienced with Him before.

I was more than ready to fight the enemy.

CHAPTER 7

My Biggest Battle Begins

"This is what the LORD says to you: 'Do not be afraid or discouraged because of this vast army. For the battle is not yours, but God's . . . You will not have to fight this battle. Take up your positions; stand firm and see the deliverance the LORD will give to you . . . Do not be afraid; do not be discouraged. Go out to face them tomorrow, and the LORD will be with you.'"
– 2 Chronicles 20:15 and 17 (NIV)

THE MORNING OF MONDAY, January 4, I met first with Dr. Barber, my general surgeon, and then with Dr. Ballard, my oncologist. Vincent and my girls accompanied me to both appointments.

Dr. Barber palpated my left breast and said that my mass was easily over 5 cm in size, much larger than the reported 3.2 cm measurement from my ultrasound two weeks earlier. He diagnosed it as T3 (out of a T1 to T4 tumor measurement scale), meaning it was larger

57

than 5 cm, but had not grown into the chest wall. He recommended preoperative chemotherapy to shrink it before his removing it via mastectomy, but said that Dr. Ballard would determine my chemo regimen. He would confer with Dr. Ballard after my exam with him. They would then jointly determine a complete treatment plan going forward.

Dr. Ballard confirmed that my tumor was over 5 cm in size; he measured it to be approximately 6 x 8 cm in size. He, too, said chemotherapy was in order given its size and aggressive nature—but that he would await my final pathology report before determining the optimal chemo regimen for me. He ordered an infusion port to be installed in my chest that week by Dr. Barber, so that I'd be ready to go for that. He also ordered a bilateral breast MRI for January 7 to obtain more diagnostic information about my tumor, as well as a whole body PET/CT scan to determine if my cancer had metastasized or spread to other parts of my body. The immediacy of all these orders told me that my cancer must be much worse than my previous diagnostic tests revealed.

The next day (January 5), both doctors received my final pathology report. It showed that my cancer was ER+, meaning it was fueled by estrogen gone haywire. ER+ is the most common type among breast cancers, accounting for 80% of those—but is typically slow growing. However, I had a ki-67 reading—the rate of cancer cell growth—

of 83%. Anything greater than 20% is considered high. Clearly, my tumor was not only large, but also *extremely* fast growing. Consequently, I was diagnosed with locally advanced Clinical Stage 3 breast cancer. Clinical Stage 4 is the highest designation for cancer invasiveness, growth and mortality.

My MRI two days later brought more bad news. In addition to the 3.2 cm mass revealed in my biopsy, two lesions on the sides of that—measuring 9 mm and 7 mm respectively—were found. Also revealed was a 5.2 x 2.6 x 1.8 cm mass located in the central part of my breast, with another smaller mass directly behind it. All were suspicious for cancer. Plus, I had several enlarged lymph nodes in my left armpit, including one measuring 2.4 cm, which indicated that my cancer might have metastasized and spread beyond my breast. Thankfully, my subsequent whole body PET/CT scan confirmed that it hadn't.

Based on this information, Dr. Ballard ordered chemotherapy to begin on Monday, January 11, just a week following my initial consult with him. Vincent and I met with him on Friday, January 8, to discuss what that would involve, as well as what treatments would follow it.

Instead of prescribing me the usual chemo regimen for patients with ER+ breast cancer, Dr. Ballard told us that he had prescribed for me—because of the super aggressive nature of my cancer—a much stronger chemo treatment typically used in patients with "triple-disease," the most aggressive and deadliest type of all breast cancers.

Accordingly, I would undergo dose-dense chemo treatment (meaning I'd have chemo every two weeks versus the standard three weeks) of a three-drug regimen called "ACT," a super-strong, highly toxic chemo combo that would be administered over a four-month period. In fact, one of those drugs, Adriamycin (the "A" in ACT), is referred to as "Red Devil," not only for its bright red color, but also for its horrific side effects, including nausea, vomiting, diarrhea, fatigue, weakness, mouth sores, and hair loss. It would be administered along with Cytoxan (the "C" in ACT), which stops bad as well as good cells from growing and has equally awful side effects. Naturally, the dose-dense treatment of these two drugs would increase the severity of their side effects. After completing four rounds of AC, I would undergo four rounds of Taxol, another anti-cancer drug.

Each chemo treatment would last from 10 a.m. until 4 p.m. Before each treatment, Dr. Ballard would measure my tumor and draw blood to ascertain my white blood cell count (WBC), which would be debilitated from chemo. If it was too low—thus risking me for infection—I wouldn't be able to undergo that day's treatment until my WBC measured within acceptable range.

Following total completion of my chemo regimen, I

would undergo total mastectomy of my left breast. After that, I'd undergo four weeks of daily radiation treatment to my left chest wall to ensure eradication of any remaining cancer cells.

This entire protocol—without reconstruction of my left breast—would take approximately ten months. That was exactly the amount of time that I needed in order to be present at my oldest daughter's wedding in Jackson Hole, Wyoming on October 3. Any delay in my treatment schedule due to low WBC readings, infections or illness would make it impossible for me to attend it. I could postpone breast reconstruction to a date after Ansley's wedding.

That might sound silly in view of the deadly seriousness of my disease, but Ansley's wedding had been planned months before my diagnosis. We had already reserved the venue, and had made hefty deposits on that as well as to the wedding planner, caterer, band, hotel, photographer and florist. Plus, we had already sent "Save The Date" notes to our invitation list. At this juncture, we simply could not change the date. While her wedding could certainly go on without me, I desperately wanted to be there for it! She was the first of my children to get married!

So, I was determined to not have any delays in my treatment! I committed myself to doing everything possible to stay as healthy as possible throughout chemo. This included exercising daily for at least 30 minutes, eating a healthy organic diet, and getting the proper amount of sleep. Because chemo depletes the body's immune system and increases risk of infection, I also limited my exposure to public environments where I could possibly contract a cold or other illness. This meant taking a hiatus from my beloved weekly Bible study at NUMC.

At the same time, I focused on my spiritual health. In addition to my daily, hourly devotional time with the Lord, I prayed with fellow believers about my healing. In fact, I pretty much prayed throughout the day! I also started devouring books on testimonies of Christians who had been healed by God from cancer, other terminal diseases, or extreme dire circumstances. I continued to listen to Christian radio stations when I was in the car. All of this built my faith in God's healing powers.

Just prior to starting chemo, Dr. Barber called Vincent. In a nutshell, he told him that I'd be physically debilitated from ACT chemotherapy. "Lisa is used to being very active," paraphrasing his words. "After this regimen of chemo, she won't have the energy to even walk to the mailbox. You need to prepare her for that." When Vincent shared this with me, I responded, "I know God is going to allow me to have a normal life during chemo." And ultimately, He did just that!

I was trying to stay positive. But admittedly, I was worried about the side effects I might suffer. Before finding my tumor, I had gone to an evening Bible study at NUMC to hear the testimony of a cancer survivor. She said she got to a point in her chemo treatment where she was so sick and debilitated from it that she just wanted to die. Losing her hair and nails were nothing compared to how horrible she felt.

I also was worried about a swollen and purple spot in my left breast at the biopsy site. It was Sunday, the day before my chemo was to begin. Any infection would preclude that from happening until it cleared. So once again, I prayed with Mary for God to take away that infection.

Later that night, I divulged my true feelings to the Almighty. "God, I know You will heal my infection so that I can start chemo treatment tomorrow," I prayed. "But I am scared to death about it. I can't do it without You. Please be with me and let me feel Your presence. Please help me to tolerate it. Please let me get through it and feel okay."

The next day, my infection was gone! I underwent my first chemo treatment as planned without incident. When I got back home, I immediately went to exercise in our gym. A friend brought dinner while I was working out and said to me, "Why am I bringing you food? You seem completely normal!" And I was—praise the Lord!

After that, I knew God was going to be with me every step of the way going forward. Accordingly, my second chemo treatment on January 25 went as well as the first. The only side effect I experienced was a mild case of mouth sores, which, in the scheme of things, was a non-event. Overall, I felt great!

God had answered my prayers.

CHAPTER 8

Dr. Ballard

"On hearing this, Jesus said, 'It is not the
healthy who need a doctor, but the sick.'"
– Matthew 9:12 (NIV)

DR. BARBER AND I WERE BOTH *very worried about Lisa West.*

We each met with this new patient for an initial consult
and exam on January 4, 2010, having been referred to us by
Piedmont Breast Center. We had received the results from her
ultrasound and mammogram, as well as the initial pathology
report from her biopsy recently performed there. Those results
were not good. They revealed locally advanced, invasive ductal
carcinoma in the left breast, with a solid mass measuring 3.2
centimeters (cm) at its widest dimension and estimated to be
Grade 3.

Upon individual examination, Dr. Barber palpated and
reported Lisa's tumor to be easily over 5 cm in diameter (thus
designated T3), and well over the 3.2 cm reported in her ul-
trasound. I measured it to be even larger: approximately 6 cm
x 8 cm. In order to obtain more diagnostic information about
her tumor, Dr. Barber ordered a bilateral breast MRI that

week; I ordered a whole body PET/CT scan to follow that.

*Her final path report received by us the next day revealed a super-elevated ki-67 reading of 83% (the rate of tumor growth; readings over 20% are considered high). Clearly, her cancer was **extremely** fast growing. Her MRI two days later revealed that in addition to the dominant mass, there were now multiple other unsuspected masses that were suspicious for additional disease, several sizeable, as well as enlarged lymph nodes suspicious for metastatic disease.*

The level and aggressive nature of Lisa's disease was truly frightening.

Dr. Barber and I agreed to get Lisa on chemotherapy as soon as possible. He installed her infusion port that same week. I prescribed dose-dense ACT therapy—one of the toughest, most aggressive chemo regimens out there—to begin on January 11.

As an oncologist with 40 years of clinical experience in treating breast cancer, including patients with Lisa's level and type of disease, I believed that she had only a 50% survival rate—even with chemotherapy and subsequent mastectomy and radiation. I was concerned about how well her cancer would respond to chemo, and also if she would be able to tolerate the brutal regimen prescribed to fight it. I didn't share this with Lisa then, as it would have been defeating. I didn't want her to be fearful of or have no hope in her treatment. There was still a good chance that it could turn the tables on her prognosis.

When I met with Lisa and her husband on January 8 to discuss her chemo protocol and other treatments going forward, she told me that she was a strong Christian and believed that God would heal her cancer. She expressed that she wasn't afraid of her prescribed chemo and its severe side effects. She said that she knew that God would help her tolerate those and remain able to carry on with all of her regular daily activities.

Ultimately, this proved to be the case.

CHAPTER 9

My Divine Healing

> *"'For I know the plans I have for you,'*
> *declares the LORD, 'plans to prosper you*
> *and not harm you, plans to give you hope*
> *and a future.'"*
> **– Jeremiah 29:11 (NIV)**

VINCENT AND I SPENT THE WEEKEND before my third chemo treatment at our farm. Ansley had flown in so that
we could work on her wedding plans. (I also think she
thought her visit would lift my spirits—and it did!) It was
late January and the depths of winter—my favorite season
there! And, for the first time in years, it was snowing heavily, which always made me happy and excited!

I was feeling great, so the three of us took a long walk
on Saturday. All the while, I felt what I can only describe
as *agape* love from the Lord. That entire day, I was filled
with an indescribable euphoric happiness and peace. At
the time, I did not understand why I had these joyful feelings in the midst of my battle with cancer.

Before going to bed that night, I was again overcome

with a feeling of overwhelming joy and love. I went to Vincent to express my feelings, while crying tears of joy. He wanted me to share this with Ansley, and she freaked out when I did! She didn't understand why I was crying if I was happy, and she thought something was wrong with me! (Something strange was definitely going on with me, but I didn't know what that was.)

Vincent and I went to bed around midnight that night with our two dogs—a Great Dane and Jack Russell terrier, who both slept on the floor in our bedroom. While trying to fall asleep (the steroids in chemo can cause insomnia), I closed my eyes and spoke silently to the Lord. All of the sudden, I had a vision of water pouring out of a faucet into a beautiful, ancient bowl. In Scripture, water represents blessings. I knew that God was giving me a vision of a blessing.

Again, all of a sudden, I heard an audible voice in my head. It was the Lord! He said, "Lisa, how many people in your Bible study have cancer?" I answered, "Three." God replied, "Name them." I told Him, "Beth, Cindy and me." He then said, "I'm going to heal all of you." To which He added, "I am also going to heal your Graves' disease, your cancer, and I will deliver your son from his struggles. Now, I want you to get up and read Psalm 3." I was so excited and overwhelmed that I was actually hearing God's voice in my head!

I replied to His request in my thoughts, saying, "I can't! I'll wake up Vincent and the dogs if I do that!" God told me that He would keep them all asleep, so I obeyed and tiptoed out of the room to read Psalm 3. I was so excited about its verses, believing God was telling me through them that He was going to help my son get through his trials.

Here is how that Psalm reads in the Bible (NIV):

LORD, how many are my foes!
  How many rise up against me!
Many are saying of me,
  "God will not deliver him."
But you, LORD, are a shield around me,
  my glory, the One who lifts my head high.
I call out to the LORD,
  and he answers me from his holy mountain.
I lie down and sleep;
  I wake again, because the LORD sustains me.
I will not fear though tens of thousands
  assail me on every side.
Arise, LORD!
  Deliver me, my God!
Strike all my enemies on the jaw;
  break the teeth of the wicked.
From the LORD comes deliverance.
  May your blessing be on your people.

God then told me to read this Psalm to my husband. I was reluctant to wake up Vincent to do this but I obediently did so, telling Vincent that God had directed me to do this. Understandably, he was a bit dumbfounded by this sudden need of mine to read Scripture to him in the middle of the night!

When I got back in bed, I heard God say to me, "Tomorrow is a sacred day. Let there be no cursing, drinking of alcohol, or anything that is not holy." (I was hardly drinking anyway, because of my cancer.)

The next morning, I called Mary to tell her about my conversations and experience with the Lord. She thought that was God's forewarning of something powerful He was soon going to do, and to be spiritually attuned to His voice and signs throughout the day. She concluded, "I'll stay close by the phone in case you need me."

Throughout that Sunday, I continued to feel the same euphoric happiness, peace and joy that I did the day before. Amazingly, it was still snowing heavily—which, for me, was a blessing from God!

That evening, Vincent, Ansley and I watched the Super Bowl, while eating Cajun Po' Boys Vincent had made in honor of the underdog New Orleans Saints playing the favored Indianapolis Colts. The game was played at Sun Life Stadium in Miami Gardens, Florida, because the New Orleans' stadium was being renovated in the aftermath of Hurricane Katrina. We were rooting for the Saints because of the horrific devastation the city experienced from Katrina. I knew in my heart that the underdog Saints would win the game—and they did! It was truly a "Cinderella" story!

All that night, I expected a call from my son, telling me that he felt wonderful and like his old self again. That call never came.

When I got in bed after the game was over around 12:30 a.m., I told God that I thought He was going to do something miraculous with my son on this sacred day. I told him I was disappointed that didn't happen, but that I was hugely grateful for the wonderful day I'd spent with my husband and Ansley, and my many other blessings. I also told Him that it was fine that nothing miraculous happened that day, because I felt so great and loved Him so much.

Right away, I heard God's voice in my head distinctly saying over and over again, "I come to prosper you, not to harm you. I come to prosper you, not to harm you." In retrospect, I know God was preparing me for what was to come that night—which could be scary without that forewarning.

All of a sudden, an overwhelming and inexplicable

force overcame me. I began to repeatedly and involuntarily rise up and down in the bed, while speaking in tongues and crying loudly.

Vincent woke up and was freaked out. He ran to get Ansley. I could hear them talking, but I couldn't manage to talk to them. Ansley held my left hand (the side of my cancer) and said that it was burning hot. Vincent held my right hand and said that it was freezing cold.

During this bizarre episode, which lasted for roughly 45 minutes, I was aware of my surroundings, but unsure of what was going on with me and unable to coherently communicate anything. When it finally stopped, we sat there looking at each other. They each asked me what happened to me. "I don't know," I replied, "but I know it has to do with God and something spiritual." Throughout this upheaval, the only ones getting rest were our dogs: they slept peacefully throughout it! That could only be God's doing, because our dogs would normally wake up and bark incessantly at the slightest noise.

Understandably, Vincent was frightened to be alone with me given my strange and out of character behavior. So Ansley got in bed with us. She and Vincent both fell right to sleep.

Just after that, I again heard God repeatedly say, "I come to prosper you, not to harm you." I sat up and again began rising up and down and rocking back and forth, while also speaking in tongues. Ansley and Vincent were up by now, pacing around the room. Vincent said to Ansley, "I think she has become mentally ill." To which she replied, "No Dad, this is something different. This is something spiritual." Ansley intuitively believed that God was with me and doing something within me.

They again each held one of my hands. As with my previous episode, they felt my left and right hand to be burning hot and freezing cold respectively. When I stopped involuntarily speaking in tongues and rocking back and forth, I reread Psalms 3 out loud to them. I then began confessing my lifelong sins to them, one after the other, from my high school years to the present. I couldn't stop. I was driven by an unstoppable compulsion to repent them all.

"Stop, Mom!" Ansley screamed. "I don't want to hear all of this." In retrospect, it was kind of funny seeing my daughter so appalled by my confessed transgressions!

By now, it was 3:00 a.m., and Vincent was getting irritated. He had an early business meeting in Atlanta. I, myself, had my third appointment with Dr. Ballard at 11:00 a.m., with chemo treatment following that. On top of that, leaders of Northside United Methodist Church were coming to the farm at 8:30 a.m., for a big meeting— and I had housecleaning to do before they arrived.

I told Ansley and Vincent, "I'll try to go to sleep, but I can't promise I can stop what is happening to me." I knew God was healing me. But I didn't know that He'd soon be back for a third and final round of healing.

The minute I laid down, that happened. I felt a dark presence enter the room. I knew immediately that it was the enemy, because it felt so evil. God immediately took over and prevailed, repeating to me His same forewarnings as before: "I come to prosper you, not to harm you." And like I responded before, I repeatedly rose up and down and rocked back and forth in the bed, while also speaking in tongues.

Vincent bolted up and said to Ansley, "I think we need to call an ambulance. I think she's gone crazy!" In my head, I heard myself saying, "No! Call Mary! She'll know what to do!" And right when I thought that, Ansley immediately said, "Dad, I think we should call Mary." God had amazingly projected my thoughts to Ansley!

Mary answered right away, and Ansley told her what had been happening. "Let me hear what's going on," Mary said. Ansley held up the phone to my mouth so that Mary could hear me speaking in tongues. Mary then said to her, "Your mother is with the Lord right now. You need to leave her be." She continued, "Please let me speak to her." Ansley then held the phone to my ear, and I heard Mary say, "Lisa, the Lord is with you right now and healing you.

Wait it through."

After that, I continued to rise up and down, and speak in tongues. When that third episode was over, it was around 4:00 a.m. Since I now could speak intelligibly to them, Vincent and Ansley felt that I had returned to "normal" and that they could safely leave me to get some sleep. Ansley retired to her bedroom; Vincent went to bed in Cubby's room.

When they left me, I wept briefly—because I suddenly felt so alone, misunderstood and rejected.

That's when I had a vision of Jesus walking along a dusty road with His heavy crucifixion cross on His back. People were throwing rocks and rotten food at him, while also cursing and yelling at Him. I realized how sad and lonely He must have then felt, having been rejected and abandoned by even His most devout followers.

Through this vision, I know God was telling me that many, including my family and close friends, would not believe or understand what I had experienced that night. God was showing me that I, too, would feel alone and rejected because of this, just as Christ did. But God did understand my feelings by revealing this vision, and that was all that mattered. Knowing this, I was finally able to fall asleep.

When Vincent awoke in the morning before leaving for Atlanta at 6:00 a.m., he told Ansley that he was very worried about me, and that he didn't understand what had happened to me. "She will be okay, Dad," she replied. She wasn't concerned or freaked out like he was.

When I got up at 6:30 a.m. that morning, I could not feel my tumor at all—not even a vague fullness of it! I knew that God had healed me!

The doorbell rang at 8:00 a.m. It was Sue Allen from Northside Methodist, who told me that the church leadership had arrived. I scurried to get ready and hit the road with Ansley to Atlanta.

On the drive back, Ansley asked me, "Mom, how do you know you're not going to have another episode." I told her I didn't—but that I knew that God had come and revealed His presence to me, spoken to and through me, and healed me. While I was elated and ecstatic about my encounter and experience with the Lord, I didn't say much more about that to Ansley or others, because I was still processing and sorting it all out in my head.

However, I would soon say that my encounters with the Lord that weekend were the most amazing, exciting and wondrous experiences in my entire life. And, the *agape* love and peace that God bestowed me during that time would remain with me forever, fortifying my trust in Him for whatever lies ahead.

When you have a supernatural encounter with the Lord, you will never forget it. Every time I think about mine, I clearly remember everything about it as if it happened yesterday. Since experiencing those two nights in the presence of the Lord with the incredible love He showered on me, I have had a wonderful sense of love and peace here on earth that I never could have gained otherwise.

Besides my Divine healing, I am a changed person from my encounter with the Lord. I never question if He can do this or that, because He instilled in me a faith that always has hope—the kind of hope that only comes from Him. From this experience, I truly believe that God will deliver on His promises and never disappoint you.

CHAPTER 10

My Mother's Miracle

"Jesus replied, 'What is impossible with man (human beings) is possible with God.'"
— Luke 18:27 (NIV)

MORE THAN NINE YEARS *have passed since I witnessed my mother's God encounter and miraculous healing. I regret that I did not record everything that occurred the night it happened. Unfortunately, my memory has faded with regards to all of that evening's details. However, I vividly remember the highlights. So, I will recount those here and now.*

It all began on what was a quiet Super Bowl Sunday night at our family's Ellijay farm. Mom had recently begun chemotherapy for breast cancer. Her doctors told us that her tumor was so large that it needed to be treated first with chemotherapy before it could be surgically removed. For clarification on its size, the doctors compared it to a Snickers candy bar. She was meeting with her oncologist on Monday, the following morning, for her third checkup with him and round of chemotherapy.

81

Mom, Dad and I spent that entire weekend in Ellijay. I'd flown in from my home in New Mexico to work with Mom on plans for my wedding in October, as well as to lift her spirits. Dad cooked us a big Cajun meal that we enjoyed while watching the Saints defeat the Colts. Shortly thereafter, we all went to bed.

After midnight, Dad woke me up and said your mother needs you. I ran to their bedroom, where she was sitting straight up in bed. She was moaning in a high-pitched scream, telling us that she "was on fire"—but not to worry because she "was with the Lord." That was easier said than done, considering that she looked like her bald head could spin off her body and that an exorcism was being performed!

Oddly, and as scary as her behavior was, I believed her explanation. Though the situation was otherworldly, I felt calm in the midst of it—unlike my father, who was beside himself with worry and asking for my advice.

As the night unfolded, I would define time in three "phases." In the first, the left side of Mom's body was on fire and she was moaning. She would barely speak to us and was mentally in a different place. After this episode, Mom asked me to sleep with her and Dad. I think that she was excited about what she had just experienced, but was also scared by it, like we were.

When we finally dozed off to sleep, Mom awoke us again

with her bizarre utterances and rocking. But this phase also included her spouting out an uncontrolled stream of confessions. As Mom's daughter, listening to her scream out her past "sins"—which I'd never before heard—was disconcerting, but also (I guiltily admit) intriguing. While she rattled off a list of her various transgressions, she tried to stop herself by closing and covering her mouth with her hands. But she was unable to quiet her words.

As her confessions wound down, we again tried to get some rest. We all turned off the lights and struggled back into bed with our heads spinning, hoping that this was the end of the evening's strange events. But the third and final phase was about to begin.

When it did, we again awoke to Mom's screaming. At this point, my father became undone, as Mom would not (or could not) communicate with us at all when we tried to talk to her. Thinking she'd gone crazy, Dad asked me more than once if we should call an ambulance. Suddenly it occurred to me that we needed to call Mary versus an ambulance, as she might know what was going on with Mom. When I told Mary the events of the evening, and let her hear Mom's utterances in the background, she assured me that Mom was okay and with the Lord.

Mom eventually calmed down and could talk to us normally. Feeling that she was now, indeed, okay, I went to my room to get some sleep and Dad did the same in Cubby's bedroom.

After getting into bed, I tried to wrap my head around the night's events. I knew that I had witnessed something mystical and otherworldly. I never doubted that my mother's experience was anything less than Divine. She was unquestionably in the presence of a Higher power. What also was amazing to me about that evening was that throughout all of its commotion, Mom's super-hyperactive Jack Russell terrier, George, slept peacefully!

When we awoke on Monday morning, Mom could not feel her tumor at all.

CHAPTER 11

My Wife's Miracle

"He is the One you praise; He is your God, who performed for you those great and awesome wonders you saw with your own eyes."
— Deuteronomy 10:21 (NIV)

IT WAS SUPER BOWL SUNDAY 2010. *I was excited because the Saints were uncharacteristically in the Super Bowl, and were the darlings of New Orleans post Hurricane Katrina. Their ascension as a team mirrored the city's rebirth after the flood. I spent much of my business career in "NOLA," and have an affinity for its people—so I was all the more invested in the game.*

I made a big New Orleans style feast, including fried shrimp Po' Boys, for the game. The Saints won, and we were all elated with their victory. It was a special time having our daughter, Ansley, back home with us—especially for Lisa, who had just started chemotherapy for a Stage 3 tumor in her left breast.

After a great night of food, fun and football, we all headed off to bed. What happened later that night will always be a blur in my memory. But at the same time, I knew that there was Divine intervention in Lisa's life that night. When I look back on that evening, I think of the movie "Men In Black," a spoof of sorts in which the main characters point a clicker at people to erase their memories of events that just occurred. I have always felt that such a clicker was pointed at me that night.

What I do remember is that sometime after we had all gone to sleep, I woke to the sound of Lisa uttering sounds and words that were not hers. Also, some of those words were not really words. I tried to snap her out of this, and she eventually told me not to worry because it was the Lord in her. After that, and still relatively early in what would turn out to be a very long evening, I asked Ansley to come to our bedroom. Lisa wanted her to sleep with us.

Lisa's strange behavioral occurrence would be repeated twice more that night—the second time, with Lisa also confessing her sins. When she returned to a normal state, she again told me not to worry; she was with the Lord. After her third "episode," Ansley called Mary, who assured us that Lisa was with the Lord and would be fine.

Eventually seeing this to be the case, Ansley and I left Lisa to finally get some sleep. I am not sure of all that happened after that. I know that I eventually went to sleep, worrying that Lisa might not return to a normal state. I had the same worry when I awoke two hours later that morning.

When Lisa and I spoke that morning, she told me in no uncertain terms that her cancerous tumor had been healed and was gone. Her state of calm that morning eased my worry and concern.

Later that morning, we went together to see her oncologist, Dr. Perry Ballard. He examined her and took a scan. After that, he was speechless and in awe of what he found: her tumor was virtually gone.

CHAPTER 12

Confirmation of My Healing

"Surely He took up our pain and bore our
suffering, yet we considered Him punished
by God, stricken by Him, and afflicted.
But He was pierced for our transgressions,
He was crushed for our iniquities; the
punishment that brought us peace was on
Him, and by His wounds we are healed."
– Isaiah 53: 4-5 (NIV)

I WAS SO EXCITED ABOUT SEEING Dr. Ballard the morning after my encounter with the Lord that I could hardly stand it! I couldn't wait to tell him about my miraculous healing!

Vincent, Ansley and my parents came with me to my Monday morning appointment. Once I was in the examination room, I repeatedly told Dr. Ballard that God had healed me, and that I could no longer feel my tumor.

He interrupted me to say that he had something important to tell me. Basically, it was that the Board of Piedmont Hospital had changed its mammography protocol because of what had happened to me. Follow-up mammograms to an abnormal one would now always include both breasts, regardless if an abnormality was reported in only one. "Our system failed you, Lisa," he said. "Because of you falling through cracks in our previous system, all of our follow-up mammograms will now always be bilateral."

I was touched by his humble admission of this, even though he was completely blameless in my falling through the system's cracks. I also realized he must have scrutinized my medical records going back to 2008, when a bilateral mammogram reported an abnormality in my right breast. The follow-up mammogram to that was only of my right breast, which was normal. "Wow," I thought. He is one great doctor truly devoted to the best possible care and treatment of his patients!

Dr. Ballard then proceeded to palpate my left breast while I was lying down. While doing this, he stared straight ahead with a puzzled look on his face. My family members were in the room, standing where they couldn't see him do this. "I'm mystified," he said. "I can't feel or find your tumor!" He continued, "This can't be . . . you've only had two rounds of chemo! It's remarkable!"

Everyone in the room began screaming for joy!

He then examined me sitting up. He said he could only feel a vague fullness in my breast, versus the rock solid mass that had been there on my previous visit. He also couldn't feel any previously suspicious lymph nodes.

"This is amazing," he said. "In fact it's miraculous!" I excitedly replied, "I told you, Dr. Ballard, that God was going to heal me—and He did!"

"I'll be right back, " he said to us. "I'm going to call Dr. Barber." Dr. Barber happened to be in surgery, but he took the call anyway (which indicated to me how concerned he was about my case).

"Dr. Barber is thrilled with this good news," Dr. Ballard said when he returned. I quickly asked, "So since God has obviously healed me, I don't have to do any more chemo—right?" To which he replied, "No Lisa. Dr. Barber and I agree that we have to make sure that your cancer is completely gone. We don't know that yet. Your chemo will continue through completion of your next two rounds of AC, starting today as planned. After that, you'll have another MRI to determine treatment going forward."

I was bummed to hear this, but understood where they were coming from and respected that. As physicians, they were professionally, ethically and morally obligated to follow clinical protocol, bringing their full arsenal of medical science, technology, and expertise to my treatment.

Dr. Ballard

Looking back today on that exam and what followed it, I can say it was truly miraculous that Lisa's tumor and previously identified lymph nodes could no longer be fully appreciated after only two rounds of chemo. I believe this was not only the result of chemotherapy, but also Divine healing. It was too remarkable to exclude the latter.

It also was truly remarkable at how well Lisa tolerated her entire course of dose-dense ACT chemo, which completely debilitates most patients. She never missed a scheduled treatment due to low WBC counts, infection, illness or severe side effects. At each physical exam before her treatments, her vital signs, constitutional systems and lab reports were all normal and/or within range, with the exception of mouth sores that were effectively treated. She always stated that she felt well and was able to carry on with her pre-disease activities, including exercising daily. She experienced no depression or mood swings.

In my professional experience, only five percent of patients tolerate ACT chemo as well as she did. There's also something to be said about how well she dealt with having and living with Stage 3 breast cancer in general. I do believe her faith in God served her well in this. And I do believe the good Lord was watching out for her.

CHAPTER 13

Faith That Moves Mountains

> *"'Have faith in God,' Jesus answered.*
> *'Truly I tell you, if you say to this*
> *mountain, "Go, throw yourself into the*
> *sea," and do not doubt in your heart but*
> *believe that what you say will happen, it*
> *will be done for you. Therefore I tell you,*
> *whatever you ask for in prayer, believe that*
> *you have received it, and it will be yours.'"*
> — **Mark 11:22-24 (NIV)**

> *"And He said to her, 'Daughter, your faith*
> *has made you well; go in peace, and be*
> *healed of your disease.'"*
> — **Mark 5:34 (ESV)**

I HAD MY HAIR CUT STYLISHLY short when chemo was initially prescribed, in order to prepare myself for losing it. It had started thinning after my first chemo treatment and completely fell out soon after that. I woke up one morning with Vincent saying, "Lisa, your hair is all over the bed!" So I proceeded to take a shower, and when I came out, I was completely bald! My Jack Russell terrier went berserk at the sight of me—yipping and yapping with fear because he didn't recognize me!

In retrospect, this was funny. But at the time, I was mortified by my image in the mirror, and started crying. Vincent immediately came to my rescue, putting his arms around me and saying, "Lisa, you are still beautiful, bald and all. Your hair will eventually grow out."

At this time, I also lost my eyelashes, eyebrows, finger-nails and toenails. Classes I attended at Piedmont Breast Center taught me how to treat and care for all of these conditions, including how to tie headscarves. I soon had a great collection of these, thanks to my sweet husband, as well as to those I made myself with my daughters' help.

These side effects of chemo were bothersome only to my vanity. I realized how blessed I was to not have experienced any of the truly debilitating side effects from my super-strong regimen of it, and to feel as good and energetic as I did after four dose-dense rounds of it. I still felt great!

Per Dr. Ballard's orders, I had a bilateral breast MRI on February 26—a week after I finished AC therapy, and a week before I would start the four rounds of Taxol in my chemo regimen. I truly hoped that my MRI would show that my cancer was completely gone, and that I wouldn't have to undergo any more chemo.

But the report proved otherwise. To summarize its major findings: "There has been substantial regression in the previously identified locally advanced left breast cancer. The dominant mass at seven o'clock now measures 1.8 cm in diameter versus 2.9 cm previously. There is a tiny mass at six o'clock measuring 0.5 cm. There is a persistent area of parenchymal distortion (dense tissue) within the central breast. Previously, there were multiple focal suspicious masses within this area. These masses are no longer discreetly evident. The previously identified suspicious left auxiliary node is not seen. No new abnormality is seen. No suspicious findings in the right breast."

Dr. Ballard was thrilled with these results when he shared them with me, saying they were remarkable. I, however, was stunned that I still had some cancer in my left breast—albeit it dramatically diminished and miniscule—because God had told me that He had healed me.

However, what Dr. Ballard didn't tell me then is that he believed that the small abnormalities reported in my MRI were not cancer! He only shared this when he was interviewed for this book, saying: *"While Lisa's MRI following completion of AC therapy reported some residual cancer, I suspected that this was dead and/or dense tissue versus cancer, as it was only vaguely palpable. At this point, in my professional opinion, I believe that her cancer had been eradicated. As her oncologist, however, I had to be medically certain of that. Therefore, I, along with Dr. Barber, recommended that her chemo continue through its completion."*

I totally understand why Dr. Ballard didn't divulge his opinions to me at that time, and why he recommended continued chemo treatment despite those. I know he was professionally bound to follow medical protocol in the treatment of my case, regardless of his professional instincts and beliefs otherwise. If he had shared those with me, I probably (or definitely) would have argued with him to stop the chemo. (I think he knew that about me!)

So . . . not knowing this at that time . . . and being humanly fearful of my mortality, I initially panicked after hearing my MRI results. I didn't understand why they showed some cancer to still be in my body. God had told me that He had healed me. I felt confused, disillusioned, disappointed, dismayed and concerned about this all at the same time.

Right away, however, Mary nipped my doubting feelings in the bud by leading me to Biblical verses in Mark 11:12-14 and 20-24. And boy, were those right on target!

In Mark 11:12-14 (NIV), Jesus was leaving Bethany on his way to Jerusalem with his disciples. On the way, he saw a fig tree with leaves, but no fruit as there should have been. Being hungry, he cursed the tree saying, *"May no one ever eat fruit from you again."* The tree did not die right then and there.

Then in Mark 11:20-24 (NIV), Jesus and His disciples left Jerusalem and came across the same fig tree, which was withered from its roots. "Rabbi, look," Peter said. "The fig tree you cursed has withered!" To which Jesus replied, *"Have faith in God. I tell you the truth, if anyone says to this mountain, 'Go, throw yourself into the sea,' and does not doubt in his heart but believes that what he says will happen, it will be done for him. Therefore I tell you, whatever you ask for in prayer, believe that you have received it, and it will be yours."*

Those verses spoke volumes to me. First, Jesus in human form had cause to be upset about things that weren't as they were supposed to be, just like I was. Secondly, Jesus as God has the power to do anything, including (metaphorically) moving mountains (or obstacles one might face). Finally, when God says He's going to answer your prayers, you need to have 100 percent faith that He will, according to His timing. Faith in God's power is a prerequisite to having Him answer the object of your prayers.

As an example of that, Mary reminded me that it took 28 years from the time the Lord told her that He would bring her husband back to her to when that actually happened. Her unwavering faith all those years that God would answer her prayers and deliver on His promises resulted in that happening.

From this, it dawned on me that God might be test-

97

ing my faith in Him with my good news/bad news MRI report. Accordingly, I reaffirmed my trust in God that He had completely healed me as He had told me He would. I resolved to press forward with total faith in that. I decided to ignore negative comments and test results from my doctors that might pull me down and destroy my faith along the way. Going forward, there was no room whatsoever for doubt.

And that "new" found gift of faith led me to what I prayed and hoped for.

CHAPTER 14

I Have Fought the Good Fight

*"... I am giving you this command in
keeping with the prophesies once made
about you, so that by recalling them you
may fight the battle well, holding on
to faith and a good conscience, which
some have rejected and so have suffered
shipwreck with regard to the faith."*
– 1 Timothy 1:18-19 (NIV)

I PROCEEDED TO COMPLETE the four rounds of Taxol remaining in my chemotherapy regimen, as both Dr. Barber and Dr. Ballard had prescribed and insisted upon. Three weeks later—on May 12, 2010—I underwent total mastectomy of my left breast and excision of three left axillary (arm pit area) sentinel lymph nodes, which were initially suspicious. Though these nodes hadn't been palpable since my February 8 appointment with Dr. Ballard, or present in my last MRI, Dr. Barber wanted them removed and examined to be sure they were benign.

The goal of my chemotherapy from the get-go was to shrink my cancer so that it could more easily be removed surgically. Yet, the pathology report from my surgery revealed no remaining cancer whatsoever in my excised breast tissue and lymph nodes! Dr. Ballard said how remarkable this was for a tumor as large and aggressive as mine was. I wasn't surprised. I knew God had healed me and that I would be cancer-free prior to surgery.

Two weeks after my surgery, I underwent daily (Monday-Friday) treatments of radiation therapy to my left chest wall for four consecutive weeks. Even though I believed that this was unnecessary at this point, my doctors insisted upon it: they wanted to be absolutely certain that not a single cancer cell remained in my body. My husband was right on board with them. Since I was still right on track for being able to attend Ansley's wedding, I went along with their wishes.

At my first post-op, follow-up appointment with Dr. Ballard in August 2010, he, in concert with Dr. Barber, prescribed a five-year course of anti-estrogen therapy with Arimidex. This drug would fight the ER+ nature of my breast cancer—and its likelihood of recurrence within five years of my initial diagnosis and treatments.

At first, I agreed to this. But within a couple of days into taking the drug, I felt a nudge in my heart. It was the Lord, telling me that He did not want me to take this drug because He had *completely* healed me. My breast cancer was *not* coming back.

I wanted to be sure that I correctly heard the Lord's instructions on this. So just as Gideon did in Judges 6 of the Old Testament, I "put out a fleece in prayer to God," asking Him for a clear, definitive sign or confirmation to show me that this was truly His will.

I got that confirmation literally within hours of when I sent out the fleece! Around noon that day, I went to get a spinach smoothie from Arden's Garden. After I ordered my drink, I heard the woman next to me say to the employee making our smoothies that she wanted to get a healthy beverage because she had cancer. I noticed this woman had no hair and was about ten years older than me. I began politely talking to her and telling her about my breast cancer experience.

She proceeded to tell me that she had been diagnosed with breast cancer four years ago. Like me, she was prescribed a medication following her surgery that would help prevent her cancer from recurring. But four years into taking that drug, she got uterine cancer! She was so upset because the drug she'd been taking per doctor's orders was supposed to keep her cancer-free. After she got uterine cancer, she researched that drug. In her opinion, she believed it was the cause of or a contributing factor to her uterine cancer.

Truly, I felt so bad for her and told her so. But at the same time, I knew that this was the sign from God that I had asked for! I began screaming right in the middle of the store with uncontainable excitement, while explaining to her about the fleece I had sent out to God that morning about my own post-surgery drug dilemma!

I believe that this encounter with this cancer victim was no coincidence or chance meeting. God was behind it, working to give me a crystal clear confirmation that I was healed and did not need to take the Arimidex. I decided right then and there that I was going to be obedient to God and be done with this drug!

I didn't tell anyone about my decision until my second post-op appointment with my doctors three months later. I knew my doctors and especially my family would be upset with my decision. There was no need for that—before, during or just after Ansley's wedding. It would have put a big damper on her big event.

My entire family and I went to Jackson Hole, Wyoming in early October to attend and celebrate Ansley's wedding. I had other cause for other celebration as well: I had accomplished my goal of finishing all of my cancer treatments in time to be present for Ansley's festivities cancer-free! I had the time of my life—with my short, now curly (formerly stick straight), grown out hair to boot!

After I returned home, I had a bone density test, which is typical for cancer patients following chemotherapy and radiation. I was hoping the results would be good, even though chemo and radiation wreak havoc on the skeletal system. Amazingly, the test's findings were consistent with normal bone mineral density. Yet another miracle!

At my second post-op appointment with Dr. Ballard in November 2010, I told him that I had stopped taking Arimidex just a few days after I had started it in August, and why I decided to do that. Understandably, he was upset with me. Even though he said he respected my faith, he reiterated the importance of my taking this drug in light of the type of cancer I had and its strong chances for recurrence. In fact, he was so concerned that he later called Vincent to discuss the matter with him.

Naturally, Vincent and my children were equally concerned and upset when they heard about this, and insisted that I take this medication for its prescribed course. I told them that I wasn't concerned or fearful, explaining that I knew God had healed me, and that healing was complete. I believed, without a shadow of a doubt, that my Heavenly Father would see to it that my cancer would not come back.

I not only got well-meaning disapprovals and berating from my doctors and immediate family about my decision, but also from my extended family and many friends. I understood where they were coming from. They were all concerned about my welfare, and didn't want me to get cancer again. Believe me, I truly appreciated their concerns and comments. At the same time, I felt that they couldn't fully comprehend or understand my position to forego medical treatment with Arimidex, and how I arrived at that. It's very hard to explain this to people who hadn't had the experiences with God that I did. So, I remained convicted of my decision.

At Thanksgiving that year, I had so very much to be grateful for—praise God! A month later, I celebrated Christmas and New Year's Eve at our family farm, just as I'd done a year ago. This time, however, I could truly enjoy the holiday season without the cloud of cancer over my head. I had come a long way in a year's time.

My Christmas card that year included, along with a wedding picture of Ansley and Rafe, the verse from Psalm 46:10 (NIV) that reads, "Be still, and know that I am God." Underneath that was a message that read: "This past year, we have much to be grateful for. Ansley and Rafe were married, and Lisa was healed of cancer."

I'll explain the significance of that verse as it related to my cancer battle, in the hopes it might help others with their battles. The word "still" in this verse comes from a Hebrew word meaning to "let go" or to "release." Through immovable faith, I let go of and released my disease (which I had no control over) to God, who did have control over it. Releasing and giving over to God our illnesses and afflictions opens the door for us to experience the fullness of all God wants for us as His creation, which includes good health. As the Bible also states, *"Dear Friend, I pray that you may enjoy good health and that all may go well with you, even as your soul is getting along well"* (3 John 1:2, NIV).

I saw Dr. Ballard for my third post-op appointment on January 12, 2011. I told him that since I had declined to take Arimidex, I didn't see the need for any further follow-up appointments with him. He was so kind, saying he was still concerned about my decision, but would respect my faith and not push the issue further. It was a bittersweet parting for me. He'd been a great doctor to me, truly concerned about my healing and recovery. We never discussed his religious beliefs, but deep down inside, I felt that he might also be a Christian believer.

I would go on to have reconstruction of my left breast in March 2011, at which time I also had a mastectomy and reconstruction of my right breast. This wasn't because I was worried about cancer appearing in my non-diseased breast—as it does in 80 percent of cases like mine. It was simply because I wanted my breasts to match in size.

It's now almost 2019—nearly 10 years after my initial diagnosis—and I've remained cancer-free to this day and writing. Thanks be to God, my Almighty Heavenly Father!

CHAPTER 15

Dr. Ballard

"You are the God who performs miracles;
You display your power among the
peoples."
                    – Psalm 77:14 (NIV)

AT LISA'S FIRST POST-OP *follow-up appointment on August 16,*
I recommended that she begin a five-year course of adjuvant
hormonal therapy with Arimidex, given that her tumor was
ER+ at 60%. I discussed the side effects of this drug with her
at that appointment.

I learned at Lisa's second post-op appointment on
November 16, 2011, that she had not been taking Arimidex
since a few days after I initially prescribed it in August. She
said that the Lord told her that He had healed her, that her
cancer was not coming back, and that she did not need to
take this medication. She has a deep faith in the Lord and
feels confident that she is permanently cured, and thus, does
not see any rationale for taking further therapy. I have tried to
convince her as forcibly as possible, without offending her, that
I felt that Arimidex is necessary in view of the ER+ nature of
her disease. I had a lengthy discussion about this with her

107

as well as with her husband, and I wasn't going to push the issue any further. She is convinced that adjuvant Arimidex therapy is not necessary. I was disappointed by this, but tried to understand and respect her religious faith with regards to this issue.

In retrospect today, I can say that Lisa made the right decision for herself in declining Arimidex therapy. It's clear that this drug was not necessary for preventing cancer recurrence in her case. Nearly nine years after I prescribed this drug, she has remained healthy and cancer-free without taking it.

As I said before, I do believe the good Lord was watching over Lisa West.

CHAPTER 16

Why Me?

> *"For He says to Moses, 'I will have mercy
> on whom I have mercy, and I will have
> compassion on whom I have compassion.'"*
> **– Romans 9:15 (NIV)**

WHY DO I THINK I WAS HEALED from cancer when other Christian believers with cancer or other potentially terminal diseases are not? I don't know the answer to that difficult question: only God does.

In fact, after I was healed, I found myself steering away from that question from those who were dying from cancer or other diseases, or those who knew people that were. I didn't know how to answer them or explain my healing. I certainly couldn't say it was because I had more faith in God than they did, or that they didn't have enough faith. And I definitely don't believe that I was special in His eyes and, thus, deserving of special attention and healing. We are all His children, and He wants the best for all of us, including perfect health.

That didn't keep me from praying to God for these

sufferers, with all my heart, for their recovery, as I continue to do today for the sick and dying.

So . . . I can only speak for myself in answer to that question. I simply believed that Jesus could heal me, just as He did countless others over two thousand years ago. I took His words from Scripture about those healings liter-ally. And, I called upon Him in constant daily prayer to do the same for me.

In my prayers to the Lord throughout my battle with cancer, I never said: "Lord if this is Your will for me to have this disease, then please help me through it." On the contrary, I knew it wasn't God's will for me to be sick or to die! I always, always, always prayed for His healing and presence with me throughout my battle.

Importantly, I was very specific and positive in all of my prayer requests, stating that I believed He could deliv-er what I asked for. One example of this is what I prayed the night before my first chemo treatment (mentioned in Chapter 7): "Lord, You know that I have an infection at the site of my biopsy that might preclude me from under-going my first chemo treatment tomorrow. I know You have the power to heal this infection, and I believe that You will do this. You also know that I'm scared to death about undergoing chemotherapy, because I don't know what to expect. Please be with me, hold my hand and let me feel Your presence throughout it. Please let me feel okay after it. I pray all this in the name of Your Son and my Savior, Jesus Christ."

God answered all of my prayer requests, according to His perfect timing.

Also, I believe that hope in God builds faith in God and His healing. The more hope we have, the stronger our faith becomes. I attained such hope and faith from certain Scripture verses that spoke to me. One is from Mark 5:34 (NIV), when Jesus says to a woman who touched His clothes in the hopes of being healed from her terminal bleeding: "Daughter, your faith has made you well; go in peace, and be healed of your disease." Another is Isaiah 55:11 (NIV), which reads: " . . . so is My word that goes out from My mouth: It will not return to Me empty, but will accomplish what I desire and achieve the purpose for which I sent it." Every time I read those verses, I visualized God speaking directly to me and it was powerful.

I would cling to and constantly reread these and other verses about God's healings. I also would reference those in my daily prayers to Him, saying "Lord, this is what You said (for example) in Isaiah 55:11 about Your promises of healing. I am counting on You to do the same for me." Doing this and having faith in the Lord is spiritual medicine for the mind, body and soul—and for me, way more powerful than mortal medicine.

So I say to those who are suffering from disease and looking for hope in God: Find scriptures in the Bible that speak to you. Hold onto them and drink them in like medicine. Repeat them over and over again until you find peace. Also, if God has told you He will heal you from your affliction, stand firm in that. Don't pay heed to negative comments or negative test results that could cause you to doubt or pull you down.

From my cancer experience, I've learned to be patient and still regarding God's answers to my prayers, knowing that He will answer those and deliver on His promises according to His perfect timing.

CHAPTER 17

A Final Revelation

"Then, leaving her water jar, the (Samaritan) woman went back to the town and said to the people, 'Come, see a man who told me everything I ever did. Could this be the Messiah?' They came out of the town and made their way toward Him."
— John 4:28-30 (NIV)

"Many of the Samaritans from that town believed in Him (Jesus) because of the woman's testimony . . . And because of His words, many more became believers. They said to the woman, 'We no longer believe just because of what you said; now we have heard for ourselves, and we know that this man really is the Savior of the world.'"
— John 4:39, 41 and 42 (NIV)

IN MY INTRODUCTION to this book, I mentioned that in the past several years, I'd had nudges from God to write it down, with a verse from Habakkuk 2:2 (NIV) that He repeatedly put on my heart. It reads: "Then the LORD

113

replied: 'Write down this revelation and make it plain on tablets so that a herald may run with it.'"

I knew that as a Christian, I had an obligation to share my story with not only believers who were suffering with life-threatening diseases, but also with non-believers—healthy or sick—who might learn from it the redemptive powers of Christ Jesus in all of life's trials. This could instill in them a desire to become a believer and follower.

That said, I never heeded those nudges to put pen to paper.

Then, in the summer of 2015, I had a "final" revelation from God on this subject (also mentioned in this book's Introduction) that convicted me to write my testimony. What follows is the account of that revelation.

I woke up on a July morning that year to see my phone showing the date as February 26. That's strange, I thought. I figured it had to be due to some kind of technical glitch with my phone or service provider. I didn't give it a second thought beyond that.

But the next morning, I woke up to my phone showing the date as February 27, instead of July something. I instantly thought that this was no technical glitch; this was God sending me some kind of message!

I had been reading *My Utmost for His Highest*, by Oswald Chambers, as my daily prayer devotional. So, I proceeded to follow what I believed was a sign from God about those two dates. I looked up in my devotional the entries for February 26 and 27.

Both were about the story of the lone, nameless Samaritan woman who encounters Jesus at the well just outside of her hometown, Sychar. Jesus was resting there on his journey to Galilee and asks the woman for a drink of water. She is shocked at that because Jews didn't associate with Samaritans. She is even more shocked when Jesus knows that she's had five husbands, and now living with a man out of wedlock. Even though she's considered a sinner and an outcast by her own people, Jesus tells her that He can give her "living water" (i.e., eternal life) whereby she will never thirst again. He then reveals to her that He is the Messiah.

This well-known Bible story is found only in the Gospel of John—John 4:4-42 to be exact. While I knew the gist of it, I proceeded to devour and study these verses.

There are many meaningful messages in these verses, including:

- God loves, values and cares about us in spite of our bankrupt, sinful lives.

- God's acceptance and grace extends to all people who believe in Him (Gentiles as well as Jews, sinners as well as the righteous, etc.).

- God actively seeks us to have a personal, intimate relationship with Him through His Son, Jesus Christ.

- Only through belief in Jesus as our personal Savior can we receive eternal life.

Those powerful messages notwithstanding, two others particularly spoke to and resonated with me. First, the Samaritan woman had a life-changing experience when she encountered the Lord and became a believer. While I was already a believer, my encounter with the Lord—though not in the flesh—also changed my life (physically and spiritually) and transformed my faith. From that point on, my faith in Him and the power of prayer has grown ten-fold. God proved to me that He was 100 percent real, and all-powerful in the healing of my deadly disease. Whenever I've started to falter in my faith, I remember to go back to Scripture, and meditate on God's words that speak to my particular issue or concern.

Secondly and perhaps most importantly, the Samaritan woman's testimony brought her townspeople to Jesus, and they all became believers as a result of that. This reinforced to me that sharing testimony about Jesus is a powerful tool in leading others to believe in Him—and that as Christians, we are called to do just that.

So this time around, I was obedient to God's loud and clear message to me: "WRITE AND SHARE YOUR TESTIMONY!" While that process took me more than three years, I finally completed the book you've just finished reading!

Praise be to God Almighty!

Acknowledgments

IT TOOK ME NEARLY THREE YEARS to write and publish this book, and I have many people to thank along the way.

First, is my lifelong friend, Elena Bennett. Elena not only believed that my story needed to be published, she also was willing to help me write it (a bonus since she happens to be a professional writer!). Her organizational skills, unwavering drive and constant encouragement kept me from being overwhelmed by the book's tasks at hand, and kept me on track in its completion.

Secondly, I want to thank Mary Office—my Christian mentor, friend and prayer partner who taught me to believe in the power of prayer, as well as how to pray. Thanks to Mary, my Christianity and faith in Jesus blossomed and grew—and continues to.

Thanks go as well to Pam Elting, a dear friend who also was instrumental in bringing me to Jesus Christ as my Lord and Savior, and in helping me to consecrate that by indirectly organizing my Baptism.

I also thank my oncologist, Dr. W. Perry Ballard, III, for agreeing to participate and be interviewed for this book. His professional perspective and opinions on the details of my disease and recovery lent enormous credibility to my story. Given how extremely busy this renowned physician is, I am all the more appreciative of the time he gave to my endeavor.

Additionally, there is Suzanne Stone—a great friend and Christian believer who knows Biblical scripture inside and out. Suzanne kindly proofread a draft of the book, checking the accuracy of its Bible verses, stories and references. Her edits and additions greatly improved the book. Suzanne also referred me to Bruce Witt, president of the Christian ministry "Leadership Revolution, Inc." An accomplished author, Bruce provided me with invaluable information on the book-publishing process, including the company that published this book.

A world of thanks goes to my sweet husband, Vincent, who not only supported me throughout my cancer journey, but also in the writing and publishing of this book. Vincent also contributed to the book's credibility by writing his eyewitness account of my Divine healing (see Chapter 11), which made the book all the more believable and powerful. I am truly blessed to have such a wonderful husband.

Finally, but most importantly, I thank my Heavenly Father. Lord, I could not live one single day without You. You have been with me since I took my first breath on earth, and You will be with me when I take my last. Thank you, Lord, for giving me my awesome testimony and story that glorifies You.

About
Dr. W. Perry Ballard, III

W. PERRY BALLARD, III, M.D., is a co-founder and practicing partner of the Piedmont Cancer Institute in Atlanta, Georgia. He is a diplomat of the American Board of Internal Medicine and is Board certified in both Hematology and Medical Oncology.

He also is a member of the Piedmont Medical Center Board of Trustees, serving as representative of the hospital's medical staff.

Dr. Ballard was born at Piedmont Hospital in Atlanta, Georgia. He grew up in Atlanta and attended The Westminster School for 13 years, graduating in 1970. He graduated from Dartmouth College in 1974, where he was elected to Phi Beta Kappa.

His grandfather, Dr. Murdock Equen, was a prominent ENT physician practicing at his own hospital on Ponce De Leon Avenue from 1930 until his death in 1966. Following in his grandfather's footsteps, Dr. Ballard graduated from Emory University School of Medicine in 1978, where he was a member of Alpha Omega Alpha.

He completed his internship and residency at the New York Hospital–Cornell Medical Center and the Memorial Sloan–Kettering Cancer Center. After residency, he did a yearlong fellowship in Infectious Disease at the Tufts–New England Medical Center in Boston, Massachusetts. He then returned to New York, where he did a three-year fellowship in Hematology and Oncology at Cornell.

At completion of his training, Dr. Ballard joined the faculty at Cornell University Medical College, where he attained the rank of Assistant Professor of Medicine. He was in the practice of Hematology and Oncology at Cornell's New York Hospital for three years prior to returning to Atlanta.

In 1987, Dr. Ballard and Dr. Charles Henderson founded Piedmont Cancer Institute, P.C, where he has since been a practicing partner.

Dr. Ballard represents the medical staff on the Piedmont Medical Center Board of Trustees. He has served as Secretary of the Medical Staff of Piedmont Hospital, as well as the Chairman of its Cancer Committee. He also has served as a member of the hospital's Advisory Board for the American Cancer Society. In addition, he has been numerously listed as one of Atlanta's "Top Doctors" in his field in Atlanta Magazine, as well as being listed in the directory of "Best Doctors in America."

About the Author

LISA WEST became a born-again Christian at the age of 40. Since then, she has organized numerous retreats, conferences and meetings for Christian clergy and counselors, as well as God-healed laypeople, to share their ministries, guidance and/or life-changing testimonies—covering everything from marriage and parenting to faith, mental illness and Divine miracles. She and her husband, Vincent, split their time between their home in Atlanta, where they were born and raised, and their family farm in Ellijay, Georgia—where Lisa experienced her encounter with the Lord that healed her advanced breast cancer. They have three children and three grandchildren. This is her first book.

About the Co-author

ELENA BENNETT has been a professional marketing-communications consultant and copywriter, as well as a personal trainer and aerobics instructor, for more than 35 years. She holds a Bachelor of Arts in Journalism from the University of Georgia, and an exercise leadership degree from the American College of Sports Medicine. Originally from Atlanta, she moved in 2017 to The Landings on Skidaway Island in Savannah, where she continues to enjoy freelance writing as well as cycling, swimming, reading and Mahjong. She is a member of Skidaway Island United Methodist Church. She has two children and one grandchild. This is her first book collaboration.

"I remain confident of this: I will see the goodness of the LORD in the land of the living. Wait for the LORD; be strong and take heart and wait for the LORD."
    – Psalm 27:13-14 (NIV)